WASHINGTON PARK BRANCH LIBRARY

DISCARDED

A SIMPLE GUIDE TO
U.S. IMMIGRATION
AND CITIZENSHIP

OTHER BOOKS IN THE ESPERANZA SERIES

(also available in Spanish)

How to Buy a House

There Is an Answer:
How to Prevent and Understand HIV/AIDS

How to Write a Résumé and Get a Job

How to Fix Your Credit

A SIMPLE GUIDE TO U.S. IMMIGRATION AND CITIZENSHIP

Reverend Luis Cortés Jr.

in collaboration with the
Immigrant Legal Resource Center (ILRC)

ATRIA BOOKS

NEW YORK   LONDON   TORONTO   SYDNEY

OCT 2 0 2008 WPK

823.6
C828S

This publication is designed to provide accurate and authoritative information in regard to the subject matter covered. It is sold with the understanding that neither the author nor publisher is engaged in rendering legal or other professional services. If legal advice or other expert assistance is required, the services of a competent professional should be sought.

ATRIA BOOKS

A Division of Simon & Schuster, Inc.
1230 Avenue of the Americas
New York, NY 10020

Copyright © 2008 by Luis Cortés Jr.

All rights reserved, including the right to reproduce this book or portions thereof in any form whatsoever. For information, address Atria Books Subsidiary Rights Department, 1230 Avenue of the Americas, New York, NY 10020

First Atria Books trade paperback edition October 2008

ATRIA BOOKS and colophon are trademarks of Simon & Schuster, Inc.

For information about special discounts for bulk purchases, please contact Simon & Schuster Special Sales at 1-800-456-6798 or business@simonandschuster.com.

Designed by Dana Sloan

Manufactured in the United States of America

10   9   8   7   6   5   4   3   2   1

Library of Congress Cataloging-in-Publication Data
Cortés, Luis, Reverend.
    A simple guide to U.S. immigration and citizenship / Luis Cortés ; in collaboration with the Immigrant Legal Resource Center.
        p. cm.—(Esperanza series)
    Includes index.
    1. Citizenship—United States.   2. Naturalization—United States.   3. United States—Emigration and immigration.   I. Immigrant Legal Resource Center (San Francisco, Calif.).   II. Title.
    JK1758.C66   2008
    323.60973—dc22   2008017519

ISBN-13: 978-0-7432-9449-2
ISBN-10:   0-7432-9449-1

Contents

Foreword

Cristina Pérez, television personality and
author of *Living by Los Dichos—
Advice from a Mother to a Daughter*

What is well learned is never lost.
(*"Lo que bien se aprende, nunca se pierde."*)

I BEGIN MY MESSAGE to you, the readers of this book, with a saying, a *dicho*, that I learned from my parents. It has guided me in
my life and I hope it will be helpful to you, too. Through hard work
and dedication, my mother and father made a life for our family—
my sister, brother, and me—and with my father's help, support,
and example, nine of his brothers and sisters eventually immi-
grated to the United States from Colombia. Our lives were full of
challenges, but our family was always full of love and I relied on
them and the love of my culture to get me through. My parents allowed us the freedom to excel in the United States, our new country, and more important, they opened doors that have given me
access to better educational opportunities and a better way of life.

The United States continues to offer immigrants many opportunities. However, immigrants also face many challenges, not the least of which is a very complicated immigration system. After the 9/11 terrorist attacks, the U.S. government has been more aggressively enforcing laws that simply do not work. We know how much immigrants have contributed to this country, yet our immigration laws today hardly consider the many benefits that immigrants have brought to the United States.

It is vitally important that you understand immigration law and how that law impacts you and your family, especially given the current environment. Since immigration is often in the news these days, with reports of new bills and provisions that make you feel afraid, it is imperative that you understand what really is happening and base any decisions you make on the best information you can obtain.

It is my hope that this book will become an essential guide for you to better understand your situation by answering many of your questions, helping you to avoid mistakes, preventing you from giving money to people who are out to enrich themselves rather than help you, and guiding you to other reliable sources of information and support. It is so important that you get a true picture of the possible impacts and implications of current immigration laws on your life and the lives of your family, friends, and community. Reliable information and an accurate understanding of immigration law will empower you and is essential for all immigrants living in the United States today.

Be sure you know what really is happening. Know the facts, and don't be fooled by someone who tells you that there is a new law when there isn't. Do not allow yourself to be taken advantage of by people who say that they can help you with an immigration problem quickly and easily, for a few thousand dollars, because they "know somebody" or for some other reason. Be a smart consumer and use the information in this book as a guide. Do not hesitate to check with experienced immigration lawyers, accredited representatives, and trusted community or religious groups and leaders. Also be aware that you can have an impact on what the government decides about immigration. The last section of this book offers some suggestions that you might consider if you want to work in support of better immigration laws.

Remember, *lo que bien se aprende, nunca se pierde.* Learn to protect yourself as a consumer and learn as much as you can about how current immigration laws can impact you and your family and what you can do about it. If you have access to a computer, please check these sites:

Esperanza USA—www.esperanza.us
The Immigrant Legal Resource Center—www.ilrc.org

Other sites to check include:

American Immigration Lawyers Association—www.aila.org
Catholic Legal Immigration Network (CLINIC)—
    www.cliniclegal.org
Central American Resource Center (Carecen LA)—
    www.carecen-la.org
Coalition for Humane Immigrant Rights of Los Angeles
    (CHIRLA)—www.chirla.org
Mexican American Legal Defense and Educational Fund—
    www.maldef.org
National Alliance of Latin American and Caribbean
    Communities (NALACC)—www.nalacc.org
National Council of La Raza—www.nclr.org

National Day Laborers Organizing Network (NDLON)—
   www.ndlon.org
National Immigrant Law Center (NILC)—www.NILC.org
National Immigration Forum—www.nif.org
Service Employees International Union (SEIU)—
   www.seiu.org

Introduction

THE ISSUE OF CITIZENSHIP and immigration has always been a center of controversy in our country. America has always been a country that not only benefits from immigration, but incorporates immigration as part of its identity. In American schools, children learn about the Statue of Liberty in New York Harbor, which says, "Give me your tired, your poor, / Your huddled masses yearning to breathe free, / The wretched refuse of your teeming shore. / Send these, the homeless, tempest-tost to me, / I lift my lamp beside the golden door!" This is the positive image of America, a country that welcomes all who would leave behind their country of origin to join this country in search of political, economic, and religious freedom.

In America today, immigration is a complex web of laws and processes. It demands of you, the immigrant, patience with a bureaucracy, a willingness to learn the process, as well as the ability to get good legal advice and support. This book is just a beginning point for you to inquire about immigration in the United States.

As a minister of the Christian faith, I want you to know that the movement of people from one nation to another for reasons of economics, famine, religious persecution, or political persecution is not new. The Old Testament, a sacred scripture to Christians, Jews, and Muslims, tells the story of the Hebrews, who, because of famine, had to migrate to Egypt. Religious persecution later forced them to leave Egypt, a land that had saved them, and cross the Red Sea back into Sinai. Christians often forget that the baby Jesus had to flee his country because of political persecution, as Herod ordered his death, and Mary and Joseph had to flee to another country to avoid their son's assassination. It is also important to point out that God understands that people will have to move from one country to another in order to survive and that the host country should and must treat immigrants with dignity and respect.

If you are a Christian, you are called to ground your conduct and treatment of others in the reading and understanding of Scripture. As such, our views on immigration are to be grounded and reared in biblical revelation. As we examine what the Bible says about immigration, we quickly encounter that the seeds for the establishment of Israel and all Christianity begin with the following statement:

> *The Lord had said to Abram, "Leave your country, your people and your father's household and go to the land I will show you."*—Genesis 12:1

The people we come to know in Scripture as Israel, and we as a Christian people, begin our history by God's ordaining immigration. It was God's call to migration and immigration that changed human history. God called one man to leave the known for the unknown, hence, to be an immigrant—an alien in a strange land. Abraham's motivation was God's call to build a great nation of promise and blessing (Genesis 12:2–3). It is a promise of something better—a better life, a better future—and it motivates sojourns into the desert in search of a better tomorrow. This is one of many immigration stories found in Scripture. It creates an understanding, a call from God to never forget this history, and requires of God's followers specific treatment of those called strangers, aliens, and immigrants. God instructs us, His people, "to love those who are aliens for you yourselves were aliens in Egypt" and to treat strangers by providing a place of rest, food, and hospitality (Genesis 18:4–5; Deuteronomy 10:19). This model of hospitality and treatment informs the development of a biblical policy regarding care for the stranger. It is a policy grounded in the actual experiences of God's people, who traveled to strange lands and who were often abused and exploited, as was the case of the people of Israel during the time of Moses. These experiences taught and required God's followers that care and treatment of the immigrant need to inform our activities in this day. The Scripture clearly says,

> *When an alien lives with you in your land, do not mistreat him. The alien living with you must be treated as one of your native-born. Love him as yourself, for you were aliens in Egypt. I am the Lord your God.*—Leviticus 19:33–34

> *Do not mistreat the alien or oppress him, for you were aliens in Egypt. Do not oppress an alien; you yourselves know what it feels to be aliens, because you were aliens in Egypt.*—Exodus 23:9

> *Cursed is the man who withholds justice from the alien, the fatherless, or the widow.*—Deuteronomy 27:19

Throughout the Old Testament, lack of fidelity to a true worship of God as expressed in the ignoring of these precepts of fairness and justice were reasons for God's judgment against His people and their impending tragedy.

In the New Testament, this theme of the treatment of aliens and strangers or immigrants is continued. We find early in the narrative that our Savior was an immigrant forced to flee to Egypt. It is this history and experience of being an immigrant people that inform the words of Jesus throughout the Gospels and are clearly expressed in Matthew 25:37. The passage teaches us about how we should treat others and it states: "For I was hungry and you gave me something to eat, I was thirsty and you gave me something to drink. I was a stranger and you invited me in. I needed clothes and you clothed me. I was sick and you looked after me; I was in prison and you came to visit me."

It is a call from Christ to all of us that are His followers to treat the alien, the stranger, the immigrant, with fairness, justice, and hospitality. It is a call grounded in years of history and personal experience. It is the same call to the care of others that God expects from His people throughout the biblical narratives. It is a call grounded in what God seeks from His children and it is to be expressed in their works today (Matthew 25:40).

If you are a citizen of the United States, what does God demand of you on this issue of immigration? How will you help make this a better and more welcoming country for those who, because of economic, religious, or political reasons, have to leave behind all that they know in order to start fresh here in America? Will you be a supporter of the traditional welcoming America or will you turn away from God's promise and demand a closed America, negating our history and God's call?

If you are struggling with your immigration status or if you know of someone who is, I invite you to read this book and become acquainted with some of the many issues you will face. Remember that this book is a primer, and because immigration is a complicated and ever-changing issue, being an immigrant in the United States today brings its own opportunities and challenges. That is why it is so important that you, as an immigrant, understand everything you can about your status and that of your family members, as well as your rights and responsibilities. It also is very important that you keep up with changes in the laws and how they are implemented, understand what these changes can mean for you and your family, and know whom you can trust to turn to for reliable and truthful information.

It is my hope that *A Simple Guide to U.S. Immigration and Citizenship* is a useful guide for you and will steer you in the right directions. It is meant to supplement, not take the place of, reliable lawyers, advisers, and religious and community leaders whom you know and trust. It also is meant to warn you away from those people who do not have your best interests at heart. Unfortunately, all immigrants today need to be careful not to be taken in by people who only want your money and, in fact, know little, if anything, about immigration. Do not allow these people to take advantage of you. They are dangerous because they can do you real harm.

A Simple Guide to U.S. Immigration and Citizenship is organized by general topics. While you can read the entire book, you should also feel comfortable focusing only on those sections that pertain to the topics of concern to you by referring to the index in the back of the book. Before you take any action based on what you read here, seek out more information by going to reliable lawyers, your religious and community leaders, and immigrant-based or community-based organizations.

Because immigration law changes frequently, it is important for you to keep up-to-date. New laws and changes in how current laws are implemented can dramatically affect you and your family.

Throughout the book, you will find Warnings and Fraud Alerts. Understanding these is an essential part of your success in dealing with your immigration status. They will help you be less likely to fall for fraudsters who may make promises that are impossible to keep, such as saying: They can get you a green card quickly. They will help keep you safe from deportation. They will inform you of your rights, because whether you're in the United States legally or illegally, you do have rights. But as the tips in this book guide you through the process, get you through the bureaucracy, and answer some of your many questions, remember that there is no substitute for an experienced attorney.

Because information really is power, it is important that you act as a wise consumer and know as much as you can about those immigration issues that impact you. That is the goal of *A Simple Guide to U.S. Immigration and Citizenship.*

1

Obtaining Legal Status in the United States

THE PROCESS OF immigration is a complicated one. But just like other worthwhile goals, attaining legal status can take a lot of work. And we're talking about more than paperwork and appointments with immigration officials.

You'll face many challenges ahead as you try to better understand and possibly change your immigration status, so you need to understand how the system works. You'll be more likely to find success if you have a working understanding of the immigration system in the United States.

This chapter will help you familiarize yourself with some important immigration terms and ideas, and you'll learn some of the ways you can get legal residence in the United States. These ideas will recur throughout the book, so remember to refer back to this chapter if you come across a term you're not sure you understand, or check the index at the back of the book.

Who in the U.S. government handles immigration?

The most important U.S. government agency you need to know about is the Bureau of Citizenship and Immigration Services, or CIS. This is the agency in charge of all immigration services that used to be handled by the Immigration and Naturalization Service, also called INS or *la migra*. These services include visa petitions, green card and naturalization applications, asylum applications, refugee applications, and more. For information about these services, visit the CIS Web site at www.uscis.gov. You can access immigration forms, filing fees, changes in immigration law, information on CIS office locations, and more.

How do I contact CIS?

If you want to speak with an immigration officer about complex immigration issues, you can make an appointment, also called an InfoPass, for a meeting at your local CIS office. You may need an appointment to discuss matters including emergency travel documents, temporary identification of lawful permanent resident status, or interim employment authorization for those who are eligible. To make an appointment, go to http://infopass.uscis.gov.

> **WARNING:** If you do not have any immigration status or immigration papers, do NOT go to your local CIS office without first consulting an experienced immigration lawyer or accredited representative. You may be exposing yourself to immigration authorities and be deported.

Who is a U.S. citizen?

Anyone born in the United States or Puerto Rico is a U.S. citizen, even if that person's parents are undocumented. Some people who are born outside of the United States inherit U.S. citizenship when they're born if that person's mother or father was a U.S. citizen.

If you're not born a U.S. citizen, you may be able to take steps to become one through a process called naturalization. Lawful permanent residents (green card holders) who meet certain requirements can apply to become U.S. citizens. If a green card holder becomes a U.S. citizen before his children turn eighteen years old, then those children may automatically become U.S. citizens, too, if they already have green cards.

> **EXAMPLE:** *Kira is a U.S. citizen. She was working in Costa Rica when she gave birth to her daughter, Marisol. Even though Marisol was not born in the United States, depending on certain requirements, she may have inherited U.S. citizenship through her mother.*

> **EXAMPLE:** *Jorge was born in San Jose, California. Both of his parents were undocumented at the time of his birth. Jorge is a U.S. citizen because he was born in the United States.*

A U.S. citizen cannot be deported or removed from the United States, except in rare circumstances where the citizenship was acquired by fraud. A U.S. citizen can petition for a parent, spouse, child, brother, or sister to immigrate to the United States.

Can you be a U.S. citizen and not know it?

Some people who were born outside of the United States may have inherited U.S. citizenship from a parent who is a citizen. People born outside of the United States who believe a parent or grandparent may have been a U.S. citizen should talk to an experienced immigration lawyer or an accredited representative to discuss the possibility.

What does it mean to be undocumented or "illegal" in the United States?

Undocumented people are those who do not currently have permission to be in the United States. The person may have crossed the border without inspection by an immigration official (sometimes referred to as entry without inspection [EWI] or present without authorization [PWA]), or the person may have entered with a temporary visa such as a student or tourist visa, and the visa has now expired, or the person may have violated the conditions of the temporary visa by working without permission or in some other way. People in the situation of overstaying their visa are often called visa overstays.

Obtaining lawful permanent residency or some other lawful status is not easy for the majority of undocumented people living in the United States. Undocumented people can face serious obstacles to getting a green card if they have traveled in and out of the United States or worked without permission in the United States. Given the complexity of the issue, it is vitally important that you consult an experienced immigration lawyer or accredited representative.

What happens if I am in the United States without papers?

Because of the unlawful presence bars, some undocumented people are hesitant to leave the United States out of fear that they will be unable to reenter, that they will forever jeopardize their ability to get a green card, or that they will have to stay out of the country for years before reuniting with family members here.

EXAMPLE: *Guadalupe is an undocumented nanny from Mexico who has lived in the United States for eight years. Her mother is*

WARNING: WATCH OUT FOR THE "UNLAWFUL PRESENCE BARS"

Undocumented people who leave the United States and try to return face serious consequences. If an undocumented person is in the United States for between 180 and 364 days in "unlawful presence" (without permission) and then leaves, he or she will be barred from reentering or getting a green card for three years. If an undocumented person is in the United States for one year or more in "unlawful presence" (without permission) and then leaves, he or she will be barred from reentering or getting a green card for ten years. If an undocumented person is in the United States for one year or more in "unlawful presence" (without permission), leaves, and then enters or attempts to reenter without permission, he or she may be permanently barred from reentering or getting a green card!

in Tijuana, Mexico, and is very ill. She would like to get permission to visit her mother and return to the United States. She is currently not eligible to apply for any lawful immigration status.

Unfortunately, Guadalupe cannot get permission to travel to Mexico and return to the United States. Permission to travel and to work is given only to people who have lawful status or, in some cases, to people who have submitted an application for lawful status. If Guadalupe asks CIS or the Bureau of Immigration and Customs Enforcement (ICE) for travel permission, they will probably deny her request and put her in removal proceedings.

However, just because a person is undocumented does not mean that he or she faces imminent deportation. Millions of people have lived undetected for many years in undocumented status in the United States, and an enormous number of American families are "mixed," containing both documented and undocumented family members. However, undocumented people are vulnerable to detention and deportation and can be picked up by U.S. government officials at any time.

Who can best help me deal with my immigration problems?

While it is good to check in with community and religious leaders, it is important that you consult with an experienced immigration lawyer or a knowledgeable accredited representative. Contact the American Immigration Lawyers Association's Lawyer Referral Service at (800) 954-0254.

What about accredited representatives?

An accredited representative works for a nonprofit organization serving immigrants and has been authorized by the government to represent people with their immigration papers. This means that an accredited representative gives you legal advice, can help you prepare your immigration applications, and can appear with you at any interviews or hearings required before immigration officials or immigration judges. In other words, an accredited representative can do much of what an attorney can to assist you in immigration proceedings and applications. An accredited representative must tell you that this is what he or she is and show you proof if you ask for it.

To find an accredited representative to help you, look for an International Institute, Catholic Charities, or other nonprofit legal services organization near you. These are reputable national organizations that help immigrants with their papers. If they can't help you, they can usually tell you about an honest lawyer or other organization near you that may be able to help. You also can seek advice from respected people in your community, such as religious and community leaders, who may be able to suggest where you can find help.

What is lawful residency?

There are three ways a person can "reside" lawfully in the United States: as a lawful permanent resident, as a lawful temporary resident, or as a lawful conditional resident. All three kinds of lawful residents can lose their lawful status and be deported or removed from the country if they do something "deportable" under the law.

What is a lawful permanent resident?

Lawful permanent residents, or "green card" holders, have the right to live and work permanently in the United States and, with some restrictions, travel outside the United States for extended periods of time. After five years (or less in some cases—see pages 111–113 for details), a permanent resident over the age of eighteen can apply to become a U.S. citizen through naturalization. A permanent resident can also petition a spouse or unmarried child to immigrate to the United States.

Permanent resident status is most commonly shown by an alien registration card. These cards are often called green cards. Permanent resident status can also be shown with a foreign passport that has a permanent resident stamp. Some people show their permanent resident status with a stamped I-94 card.

What is a green card?

A green card is a U.S. permanent resident card. It is a noncitizen's proof that he or she has permission to permanently live and work in the United States. The card includes the permanent resident's name, photograph, alien registration number (often called an A number), birth date, and other information. Permanent residents in the United States must carry their green cards with them at all times.

Many Spanish speakers refer to a green card as a *mica*. Depending on where you live, having a *mica* could mean having permanent resident status (a green card), having a work permit, or having only a border crossing card, which is valid for seventy-two hours. However, in English, having a green card specifically means having lawful permanent residency status.

In case you're wondering, green cards got their name from their original color, but they're not green anymore.

You'll read more about the different ways to get a green card later in this chapter.

What is a lawful temporary resident?

Lawful temporary residents are people who are in the process of getting legal status through one of the former "amnesty" programs. There are not many lawful temporary residents around anymore because most already have become lawful permanent residents.

What is a lawful conditional resident?

Lawful conditional residents are people who got their green cards through a spouse within the first two years of marriage. They can be eligible to become full-fledged permanent residents after a two-year "testing period." During this two-year period, conditional residents can receive most of the benefits that lawful permanent residents do. They can work, travel in and out of the United States, and count the time they spend as conditional residents toward the requirements for U.S. citizenship. They are given a green card similar to the regular green card except that it has an expiration date of two years from the date of issuance. Near the expiration date, they must apply to have the conditions on their lawful residency removed so they can become lawful permanent residents.

What is a visa?

A visa allows a person to travel to the U.S. border to ask an immigration officer to allow entrance into the country. A visa does not necessarily permit entry into the United States. Only the immigration officer has the authority to permit entry and to decide the length of stay for any particular visit.

There are two categories of U.S. visas: immigrant and nonimmigrant.

What are immigrant visas?

Immigrant visas are granted to people who are coming to the United States and are eligible for a green card. People with immigrant visas use this visa at the border to enter the United States. Once they enter the country, they are permanent residents. People with immigrant visas also use their visas when they are inside the United States, for example, as proof that they are eligible to work legally.

Each year the U.S. government issues 140,000 "employment based" permanent visas. These go largely to people who are sponsored by their employers and have permanent offers of employment in the United States.

What are nonimmigrant visas?

Nonimmigrant visas give people the right to enter and remain in the United States temporarily for a specific purpose. Some nonimmigrant visas can lead to permanent resident status, but most do not. Some nonimmigrant visas allow the visa holder to work legally in the United States, but many do not.

People usually must apply for a nonimmigrant visa at their nearest U.S. consulate in their home country.

If people are already in the United States on one kind of nonimmigrant visa, they can change to another nonimmigrant visa category without having to leave. There are some restrictions on changing visa categories, so it's important to consult an experienced immigration lawyer or accredited representative before one's current status expires.

What are the different kinds of nonimmigrant visas?

There are many different kinds of nonimmigrant visas.

- **A:** Diplomatic employees and their households.
- **B:** Business visitors (B-1) or tourists (B-2). These are granted to visit the United States temporarily for business or pleasure. This visa generally is issued for six months and can be extended up to one year. To be approved for a B visa, you must show that you have no intention of coming to the United States permanently by showing work, family, and social ties to your home country.
- **C:** Aliens in transit (pass-through at an airport or seaport).
- **D:** Crewmember (air or sea).
- **E:** Treaty investors or treaty traders (from countries where we have a treaty of commerce and investment).
- **F:** Students. These visas are granted to attend a nonvocational school, college, university, language program, or art school as a full-time student. These visa holders have limited ability to work legally in the United States and the visa does not lead to eventually getting a green card.
- **G:** Employees of international organizations (International Monetary Fund [IMF], Overseas Private Investment Corporation [OPIC], Organization of American States [OAS], International Red Cross, etc.).
- **H:** Temporary workers. These are granted to the following professionals: professionals in specialty occupations (H-1B),

nurses (H-1C), seasonal agricultural workers (H-2A), temporary or seasonal workers, nonagricultural, service sector work (H-2B), or trainees (H-3), and people from Canada and Mexico on special projects (TN visas).

- **I:** Representatives of international media.
- **J:** Exchange visitors, including educational exchange students, au pairs, graduate medical trainees, practical training students, professors and researchers, short-term scholars, camp counselors. These are for people who come to the United States to work, study, or receive training. Upon completion of their training, many of them must return to their home countries before they can change their immigration status or get a green card.
- **K:** Fiancés and fiancées; spouses of U.S. citizens married abroad. These people are granted temporary status and eventually can get a green card. They also include the fiancé(e)'s children, or the children of the spouse of a U.S. citizen who are waiting outside of the United States for the approval of an immigrant visa petition.
- **L:** Intracompany transferees (executives, managers, persons with proprietary knowledge).
- **M:** Language and vocational students. These are granted to people who attend a specific educational or vocational program such as flight school or cooking school. M visa holders cannot work and can accept only practical training after their studies are completed.
- **N:** NATO employees.
- **O:** Extraordinary ability aliens.
- **P:** Athletes, entertainment groups (such as orchestras), and support personnel.
- **Q:** Cultural exchange visitors (e.g., participants at the Washington, D.C., Smithsonian Folklife Festival and performers at

the Disney's Epcot Center Mexico Pavilion).

- **R:** These are for ministers and other professional religious workers. The visa is valid for three years and can be extended an additional two years.
- **S:** Criminal informants. People who are working with the attorney general's office on a criminal investigation or prosecution of a criminal organization or enterprise may receive this visa.
- **T:** These are for victims of a severe form of trafficking in persons. These people are granted this visa because they are living in the United States as victims, and would suffer extreme hardship involving unusual and severe harm if removed. This visa also is available to the trafficking victim's spouse and children (and parents if the victim is under twenty-one years old). T visa holders are eligible to get a green card after three years.
- **TN:** NAFTA professionals.
- **U:** These are for victims of criminal activity, and for people who have been helpful in a law enforcement investigation or prosecution of a crime and have suffered substantial physical or mental harm as a result of the crime. The crimes that qualify victims for this visa include domestic violence, felonious assault, prostitution, torture, incest, rape, sexual assault, kidnapping, and abduction. Some victims' spouses, children, and siblings will also qualify for the visa. U visa holders are eligible to get a green card after three years.
- **V:** Spouses and minor children of permanent residents who are waiting for green cards. These people are granted a temporary status and permission to work, are protected from deportation, and eventually can get a green card. The V visa is available to the spouses and minor children of lawful permanent residents who have been waiting to immigrate through a

petition filed by their permanent resident relative for at least three years. The permanent resident family member must have filed the visa petition before December 21, 2000.

What other kinds of status are there?

There are many other kinds of legal status that allow people to live and work in the United States. Some are temporary and do not necessarily lead to people becoming permanent residents, while others allow people to become permanent residents, and then if they so choose, to apply to become citizens. These include:

- **Asylees and Refugees:** These are people who have been granted political asylum or refugee status and who have not yet become permanent residents. They have the right to work, to travel outside of the United States, and to accept certain public benefits. They are also eligible to eventually become permanent residents.
- **Deferred Action:** This is granted to people due to compelling circumstances. The most common recipients of deferred action are abused spouses and children with approved immigration self-petitions under the Violence Against Women Act (VAWA). Deferred action does not lead to a green card. However, approved VAWA self-petitioners are separately eligible to get a green card.
- **Parolees:** These are people who CIS and/or CBP (Customs and Border Protection) have allowed into the United States for a variety of reasons. People may receive parole status because they have serious medical conditions that require treatment in the United States or are important witnesses in criminal proceedings. Being granted parole does not lead to getting a green card.
- **Temporary Protected Status (TPS):** This is a temporary im-

migration status. It does not lead to a green card and is granted to people from countries that the United States considers too dangerous to return to because of ongoing armed conflict (places such as Liberia and Somalia), environmental disasters (such as when huge earthquakes hit El Salvador in 2001 and Hurricane Mitch hit Honduras and Nicaragua in 1998), or other extraordinary and temporary conditions. If a country receives a TPS designation, some people from that country who already are in the United States may remain here and receive work authorization for a temporary period of time. Those who receive TPS must reregister for TPS annually.

As of early 2008, TPS designated countries are Burundi, El Salvador, Honduras, Nicaragua, Somalia, and Sudan.

What are some ways to immigrate to the United States and get a green card?

There are many different ways people become lawful permanent residents. Some of the most common ones are discussed below.

- **Family-based immigration:** The vast majority of lawful permanent residents immigrate to the United States through a U.S. citizen or lawful permanent resident family member. You'll find the eligibility requirements and an explanation of the process later in this book.
- **Employment-based immigration:** Some foreign workers who have unique job skills and a job offer from a U.S. employer can obtain lawful permanent residency if they can show that they will not displace an American worker or have extraordinary ability. You'll find the eligibility requirements and an explanation of the process later in this book.
- **Asylee and refugee status:** People who have been persecuted

or may be persecuted in their home countries because of their race, nationality, political beliefs, membership in a particular social group, or religion and are determined to be asylees or refugees can obtain lawful permanent residency. Eligible asylees and refugees must be able to show that they fear harm from the government in their home country or harm from a group that the government is unwilling or unable to control (for example, guerrillas or death squads).

- **Cancellation of removal:** Individuals who are in removal proceedings can have their removal from the United States canceled by an immigration judge if they have been in the country continuously for ten years or more, have "good moral character," and can show that their deportation would result in exceptional and extremely unusual hardship to their U.S. citizen or lawful permanent resident spouse, parent, or child. Individuals who are granted cancellation of removal obtain lawful permanent residency.

FRAUD ALERT: Be careful if someone tells you that it is easy to get a green card if you have been in the United States for ten years. This is a lie and a common scam.

- **Diversity visa lottery:** Winners of a visa lottery among countries with low immigration to the United States can obtain lawful permanent residency. The green card lottery, officially called the Diversity Visa Lottery Program, gives out fifty thousand immigrant visas per year to people from countries with low rates of immigration. The countries include those that have sent fewer than fifty thousand immigrants to the United States in the past five years. People from Canada, China, Colombia, the Dominican Republic, El Salvador, Haiti, India,

Jamaica, Mexico, Pakistan, the Philippines, Poland, Russia, South Korea, the United Kingdom, and Vietnam cannot participate because they come from countries that have sent more than fifty thousand immigrants to the United States in the past five years.

In order to qualify, one must a) be from a country that is able to participate in the visa lottery, b) have a high school diploma or equivalent or two years of certain kinds of work experience, and c) apply to enter the lottery. There is no fee to apply. You may also apply from within the United States. The application must be submitted online during the set registration period, which is usually in the autumn months. Winners are chosen randomly from all of the qualified entries and are allowed to bring their spouse and any unmarried children under the age of twenty-one.

- **NACARA for Nicaraguans, Cubans, and Former Soviet Bloc Nationals:** The Nicaraguan Adjustment and Central American Relief Act of 1997 (NACARA) provides permanent residency to nationals of Nicaragua or Cuba who have been physically present in the United States since December 1, 1995, are admissible, and filed the application for permanent residency before April 1, 2000.
- **Relief for Haitians:** Haitian nationals who were present in the United States since 1995 and filed applications before 2000 are eligible for permanent residency under the Haitian Refugee Immigration Fairness Act of 1998 (HRIFA).
- **Registry:** People who have lived continuously in the United States since January 1, 1972, may apply for lawful permanent residence under the registry program. To qualify, they must be "admissible" and must be able to establish "good moral character."

Someone who is "admissible" can lawfully enter the United States after inspection or permission by an immigration officer. Noncitizens need to be admissible every time they make an admission into the United States, apply for a green card, or apply for a visa. Immigration law contains a list of things that would make someone inadmissible, some of which you can find later in this book.

- **Violence Against Women's Act (VAWA):** People who are eligible to immigrate through a U.S. citizen or green card holder spouse, parent, son, or daughter but can't because that family member is abusing them can petition for themselves to immigrate to or to remain in the United States and apply for a green card on their own petition. See chapter 2 for more on the VAWA.

2

Getting Help from Your Family

F OR SOME HOPEFUL immigrants, family members can be a valuable resource in the journey to be in the United States legally. But there are many rules, and not every family member can be of help to you. This chapter will show you what relatives can and can't do for you.

Can my family member in the United States petition for me to come here so that I can eventually get a green card?

U.S. citizens and lawful permanent residents (persons with green cards) can help certain family members immigrate to the United States by submitting a family petition on their behalf. U.S. citizens can help their spouses, their children (regardless of their marital status), their siblings, and their parents to immigrate here. Lawful permanent residents can petition for their spouses and unmarried children.

Obtaining a green card (acquiring permanent residence)

through a family member is a two-step process. In the first step, the U.S. citizen or lawful permanent resident files a petition for the family member. In the second step, the immigrating family member files an application for a green card.

WARNING: U.S. citizens and lawful permanent residents can petition ONLY for the family members listed below:

WHO CAN PETITION FOR WHOM?

U.S. Citizens Can Petition for:	Lawful Permanent Residents Can Petition for:
Spouse.	Spouse.
Unmarried children under the age of 21.	Unmarried children under the age of 21.
Unmarried sons and daughters over the age of 21.	Unmarried sons and daughters over the age of 21.
Married children under the age of 21.	
Married sons and daughters over the age of 21.	
Parents (if the U.S. citizen is over 21).	
Siblings (if the U.S. citizen is over 21).	

If the U.S. citizen or lawful permanent resident is abusive, the family member may be able to *self-petition* under the Violence Against Women Act (VAWA), discussed later in this chapter.

Can family members with nonimmigrant visas help?

In some cases, the spouses and minor children of nonimmigrant (temporary) visa holders can come to the United States with the primary visa holders. (These spouses and children must fall under the immigration definition of *spouse* and *child* as described below.) They can apply at the same time as the primary visa holders, or they can apply later. The spouses and children of the visa holders are not necessarily allowed to work or study in the United States, even if the primary visa holders are. Spouses of visa holders will lose their visa status if the marriages terminate. And, if the principal visa holders become deportable or otherwise violate the provisions of the visa, they—as well as the spouses and children—will lose their status.

What is the first step?

To get a petition approved, the family must prove that the person submitting the visa petition (the "petitioner") is a U.S. citizen or lawful permanent resident, and that the family member who wants to immigrate (the "beneficiary") has the required family relationship to the petitioner. In order to prove a required family relationship, it's important to understand that immigration law has its own definitions for family relationships.

Who is a "spouse" under immigration law?

A person immigrating through a U.S. citizen or permanent resident as a spouse must demonstrate two things: that the marriage is both valid and legal and is bona fide (not a fraud). A couple is legally and validly married if the marriage is recognized as valid in the place where the couple was wed, and the couple was free to marry each other. If either spouse was married before, he or she must present proof that the prior marriage was legally terminated before being married again.

EXAMPLE: *Maribel and Ernesto have been together for over ten years. They have three children, have lived in California the en-*

tire time they have been together, and together own a home and a business. They had a wedding ceremony in a church but neither applied for a marriage license or ever legally married. They consider themselves married and most of their friends and family think that they are married.

Maribel has a green card and wants to petition for Ernesto so that he can obtain a green card. However, in California a couple must be legally married in order to be considered married. Living as a "common law" married couple is insufficient and thus, for the purposes of immigration law, Ernesto is not Maribel's husband.

So-called common-law marriages would qualify someone as a spouse for immigration purposes only in the following states: Alabama, Colorado, Kansas, Rhode Island, South Carolina, Iowa, Montana, Oklahoma, Texas, the District of Columbia, and, in certain cases, Pennsylvania and Utah.

Married couples also must meet a specific test to show that their marriage is real and not entered into just for immigration purposes. They must demonstrate that at the time they were married, their goal was to create a real marriage relationship and not to commit immigration fraud. The penalties for submitting a family-based petition based on fraud are very severe and include a possible jail sentence, deportation, and a permanent bar from ever getting a green card.

EXAMPLE: *Juan Miguel and Laura became good friends in college. As graduation neared, Juan Miguel realized he would have to return to Mexico with the expiration of his student visa. Although they were not a couple, Laura offered to marry him to help him get a green card. She figured there would be no harm in marrying Juan Miguel temporarily so he could stay in the United States.*

They got married at city hall and, to make the marriage appear more believable, lived together after they got married. While living together, Juan Miguel and Laura fell in love and decided they wanted to stay together. Later, when Laura submitted the family-based petition for Juan Miguel, they faced a real problem because at the time they got married they did not have a bona fide marriage. CIS (Citizenship and Immigration Services) takes marriage fraud (getting married for an immigrant benefit) very seriously and will be searching for signs of it in Laura's petition for Juan Miguel and Juan Miguel's immigration interview. If CIS finds that Laura and Juan Miguel committed marriage fraud, then Juan Miguel may be deported and forever prevented from getting a green card.

What is a "child" under immigration law?

The definition of a "child" under immigration law includes:

- Natural children born in wedlock.
- Stepchildren, whether born in or out of wedlock, if the marriage creating the step-relationship occurred before the child's eighteenth birthday.
- Adopted children if the adoption was finalized before the child's sixteenth birthday and the child has been in the adoptive parent's physical and legal custody for two years.
- The child is an orphan and was adopted, in which case there are more lenient rules.
- Children born out of wedlock. If the petitioner is the father, it must be shown that the child is legitimated or acknowledged by that father.

To be petitioned by a family member as a "child" under immigration law, the child must be unmarried and under twenty-one years of age.

WARNING: ADOPTION BY A U.S. CITIZEN DOES NOT GUARANTEE U.S. CITIZENSHIP

Children who are adopted by U.S. citizens automatically become U.S. citizens *only* if certain requirements are met: They must be adopted before they turn 16 AND be in the adoptive parents' legal and physical custody for at least two years; they must still be under the age of 18; and they must have a green card.

EXAMPLE: Elena was undocumented. A U.S. citizen adopted her when she was 14. Her U.S. citizen parent filed a family-based immigration petition for her, and Elena became a permanent resident when she was 17. At the same moment that she became a permanent resident, she also automatically became a U.S. citizen because on the day she became a permanent resident, she had also already been adopted before age 16, and had resided for two years in the legal and physical custody of her U.S. citizen parent.

What are "sons and daughters" under immigration law?

Once the child of a U.S. citizen or lawful permanent resident turns twenty-one years old or gets married, that child is no longer considered a "child" for immigration purposes and instead is now a "son" or "daughter." This is an important distinction because eligibility for a green card and/or the wait to obtain a green card may be vastly different for a "child" than it is for a "son" or "daughter."

EXAMPLE: *Nora is a lawful permanent resident. Four years ago she filed a family-based petition for Carlos, her twenty-five-year-*

old son. Unmarried sons and daughters of lawful permanent residents currently must wait for more than ten years after the approval of their family-based petitions before they can obtain a green card. Therefore, Carlos must wait in his home country until he can apply for his green card. Last week, Nora received a letter from her son telling her that he and his girlfriend got married on a recent romantic getaway weekend.

Unfortunately, Carlos is no longer eligible to immigrate through his mother, Nora, because lawful permanent residents, unlike U.S. citizens, cannot petition for their married sons or daughters. Nora will have to become a U.S. citizen in order to continue helping Carlos immigrate.

What are "siblings" under immigration law?

People are considered siblings when they have the same parents. A sibling (brother or sister) relationship also exists in immigration law when the siblings share at least one parent.

> **EXAMPLE:** *José and Carlos have the same mother but different fathers. They are considered siblings for immigration purposes.*

What are "immediate relatives" under immigration law?

Immediate relatives include:

- Spouses of U.S. citizens.
- Parents of U.S. citizens if the U.S. citizen sons or daughters are twenty-one years of age or older.
- Unmarried children under twenty-one years of age of U.S. citizens.

Immediate relatives can obtain their green cards quickly because they do not have to wait to apply for one. They need to wait only for the amount of time it takes the immigration authorities to process their application. There also is no limit on the number of people who can get green cards if they qualify as immediate relatives.

No family members of permanent residents are considered immediate relatives under immigration law. Thus, all family members of lawful permanent residents with an approved family-based immigration petition will have to wait for some period of time before they can apply for a green card. These waiting periods result from a cap on the number allowed each year in each category (see preference categories on page 31) and processing delays.

What happens if I file for my relatives too soon?

If you submit an immigration application—such as an application for a green card—before you are eligible, CIS will reject the application and send it back to you.

Can I live legally in the United States and get a work permit after my visa petition is approved?

No, the fact that the CIS approves your family-based immigration petition does not necessarily give you the right to live or work in the United States while waiting to apply for a green card. An exception to this prohibition is provided through the V visa (see page 27). Also, some immediate relatives will be able to live and work legally in the United States while they wait for the green card.

What are the possible consequences if I work or live in the United States without permission while I am waiting to apply for a green card?

The immigration laws say that you could be picked up by immigration officials and deported at any time while you are living or

WHAT IS THE VIOLENCE AGAINST WOMEN ACT?

VAWA allows abused spouses, children, and parents of U.S. citizens and lawful permanent residents to obtain work authorization and public benefits and remain in the United States, as well as lawful permanent resident status. U.S. citizens and lawful permanent residents can petition for certain family members through a "family visa petition." However, in some abusive family relationships, the family member with lawful status uses immigration status to exert control over his or her undocumented family members by threatening to call the immigration authorities and refusing to file the necessary immigration paperwork. VAWA permits an abused spouse or child of a U.S. citizen or permanent resident or an abused parent of a U.S. citizen son or daughter to *self-petition* for lawful immigration status without the knowledge or cooperation of the abuser.

WHAT ARE THE REQUIREMENTS TO SELF-PETITION UNDER VAWA?

- The abuser is or was a U.S. citizen or lawful permanent resident.
- The abuse meets the immigration definition of battery or extreme cruelty.
- The self-petitioner lived with the abuser at some point in time.
- The self-petitioner is a person of good moral character.
- If self-petitioning as a spouse:
  - The self-petitioner is or was legally and validly married to the abusive U.S. citizen or permanent resident.

- The marriage was a "good faith" marriage and was not solely entered into in order to obtain an immigration benefit.
- The abuse occurred during the marriage.
- If self-petitioning as a child:
  - The self-petitioner must qualify as a "child" under immigration law.
  - Some children may qualify for VAWA even if they were not abused, if they are the derivative of a parent's VAWA self-petition.
- If self-petitioning as a parent:
  - The abuser is or was a U.S. citizen (parents of abusive lawful permanent residents do not qualify).

working in the United States without permission. You have no rights to your job, so you could be fired, and you may be ineligible for a green card later.

What is the V visa?

The V visa provides one of the very few ways by which a person with an approved family-based immigration petition may legally live in the United States and be authorized to work before being eligible to apply for a green card.

Spouses and children (who are unmarried and under twenty-one) of permanent residents whose family petitions were filed on or before December 21, 2000, and who have been waiting for three years or more may apply for the V visa whether they are living in or outside of the United States and whether they are in or out of status. Once the visa is granted, they will be given permission to reside and work in the United States for up to two years at a time. V visa holders need to extend status in order to remain eligible for adjustment of status.

> **EXAMPLE:** *Carmelo filed for his wife, Josefina, in November 2000. In November 2003, Josefina became eligible to apply for a V visa, thereby granting her permission to reside and work in the United States.*

In order to qualify for the V visa, a child has to be eligible for the visa when he or she reaches the three-year mark, not just as of December 21, 2000.

> **EXAMPLE:** *Carmelo filed for his daughter in November 2000 when his daughter was twenty years old. Her visa was pending for the required three years in November 2003. However, because she was over twenty-one by that date, she was ineligible for a V visa.*

> **EXAMPLE:** *Andrea filed for her son on December 15, 2000. Andrea's son was seventeen at the time. His visa was pending for the required three years in December 2003. At that time, he was twenty, so he was still eligible for a V visa. He can remain in V visa status until he is eligible to get a green card, even if he turns twenty-one first, because at the time he applied and got the V visa, he was under twenty-one, and as long as he remembers to extend his V visa status before it expires.*

What are the benefits of getting a green card?

The benefits of obtaining a green card are enormous, including the right to live and work permanently in the United States and the right to petition for your spouse and unmarried children.

There are two main ways to become a permanent resident/ obtain a green card. One, called adjustment of status, is a process that occurs within the United States. Only certain people are eligible to adjust status. The second way is called consular processing, and it requires the applicant for a green card to travel to his or her home country and attend an immigrant visa interview at the U.S. consulate there.

WARNING: The V visa does not provide an automatic path to a green card for those undocumented people who received this visa but resided in the United States for more than 180 days. If you are in this situation, you should consult with an experienced immigration lawyer or accredited representative before applying for a green card.

WARNING: TELL CIS IF YOU CHANGE YOUR ADDRESS

The law says that you must notify CIS within ten days if you change your address. You do this by filing Form AR-11 with CIS. The form can be downloaded from the CIS Web site at www.uscis.gov and includes an address for filing the form. If possible, send the AR-11 via certified mail, return receipt requested, and make a copy of the AR-11 as proof that you filed the form. It is especially important to notify CIS of your change of address if you have an application pending with them, so you can be sure that any notices that CIS sends reach you. If you have an application pending with the CIS, you MUST file a change-of-address form with BOTH the office address on the form AND with the CIS office where your application is pending. If you don't, you will not receive the information you need and your application could be denied.

What are the requirements to get a green card through a family-based petition?

If you have an approved family-based immigration petition, your next step is applying for a green card. You file your application for the green card for yourself. You will need to submit certain documents, photographs, and immigration forms and pay certain fees that are associated with the forms. You will also need to have your fingerprints taken, take a medical exam, and show that you are not inadmissible (there's a list of things that might bar someone from entering the United States and getting a green card, or render them inadmissible, which is discussed later in this chapter).

Some people are able to obtain a green card very soon after the family-based petition is approved. Others may have to wait up to ten or twelve years or more before they can even apply for a green card. How long the person must wait depends upon a number of factors, including what country the person was born in and what kind of family-based petition was submitted. These variations are known as preference categories, and they're discussed in detail below.

Finally, you will have to go to an interview.

What are the "preference categories"?

If you are not an immediate relative (the spouse, parent, or child of a U.S. citizen) and have a valid, approved family-based immigration petition, you would fall under one of the different preference categories. People in the preference categories almost always face longer waits to get a green card than do immediate relatives because there are only a limited number of spots annually available in each family category. Please note that there are not categories for all relatives. For instance, there is no category through which an uncle or cousin could immigrate to the United States.

There are four different preference categories, each with different waiting times:

- **First Preference Category:** The first preference is made up of the unmarried sons or daughters, twenty-one years of age or older, of U.S. citizens. Depending on their country of origin, people in the first preference must wait between about six and sixteen years before they can apply for a green card. There are 23,400 available annually.

  EXAMPLE: *Elizabeth is twenty-three years old and unmarried. Her mother is a U.S. citizen. Elizabeth would be in the first preference category instead of an immediate relative because she is over twenty-one years old.*

- **Second Preference Category:** The second preference is made up of family members (spouses and children and unmarried sons and daughters of legal permament residents). There are 114,200, visas available annually, plus the number (if any) by which the worldwide family preference level exceeds 226,000, and any unused first preference numbers. There are two subcategories in this preference: the 2A and 2B categories:

  —*2A Category:* The spouses and children (unmarried and under twenty-one) of a lawful permanent resident. Depending on their country of origin, people in the 2A category must wait about five years before they can apply for a green card.

  —*2B Category:* The unmarried sons and daughters, twenty-one years of age or older, of lawful permanent residents. If you are a son or daughter of a permanent resident and you get married before you obtain your own green card, you will be ineligible for a green card under this category. People in the 2B category must wait between nine years and sixteen years, depending on their country of origin, before they can apply for a green card. This category is 23 percent of the overall second preference limitation.

Example: Carlos, age thirty and unmarried, has a lawful permanent resident mother. If Carlos gets married, he would be ineligible to get a green card through his lawful permanent resident mother.

- **Third Preference Category:** The third preference is made up of the married sons and daughters, of any age, of a U.S. citizen. Depending on their country of origin, people in the third preference category must wait between about eight and seventeen years before they can apply for a green card.

  EXAMPLE: *Maria is forty-five years old, married, and her mother is a U.S. citizen. Maria falls in the third preference category.*

- **Fourth Preference Category:** The fourth preference is made up of the brothers and sisters of U.S. citizens. Your U.S. citizen brother or sister in this case must be at least twenty-one years old. Both you and your U.S. citizen brother or sister must at one time have been the children of at least one common parent. The amount of time people in this category must wait before they can apply for a green card currently is between about eleven and twenty-two years, depending on their country of origin.

What is a priority date?

If you're immigrating through the preference categories, the date on which the CIS *receives* the I-130 visa petition that your family member files for you becomes your priority date once CIS approves the petition. (Keep in mind that you may receive a notice from CIS that they received your petition but you may not receive an approval notice for months or even years.) Your priority date is very important: It establishes your "place in line" and therefore how long you will have to wait before you can submit your application for a green card.

> **FRAUD ALERT:** Beware of anyone asking you for money in exchange for cutting the time you need to wait to get your green card. Such a person may be a fraud, and this is a common scam.

The Department of State (DOS) has created a chart, called the visa bulletin, that indicates how long people in the preference categories must wait before they can get their green cards. This chart is updated monthly and lists priority dates for the different preference categories and countries. There is one priority date (which can change monthly) for each preference category for most countries. On the following page is some of the information from the June 2008 visa bulletin.

The priority date listed for your preference category and country will indicate if you're eligible to apply for a green card. If your priority date is before the date listed on the visa bulletin, then you may apply for a green card.

Preference Category	All countries except China, India, Mexico, and the Philippines	China— mainland born	India	Mexico	Philippines
1st	Mar. 15, 2002	Mar. 15, 2002	Mar. 15, 2002	July 22, 1992	Mar. 15, 1993
2A	July 15, 2003	July 15, 2003	July 15, 2003	May 1, 2002	July 15, 2003
2B	Aug. 1, 1999	Aug. 1, 1999	Aug. 1, 1999	Apr. 8, 1992	Feb. 22, 1997
3rd	June 8, 2000	June 8, 2000	June 8, 2000	Aug. 1, 1992	Apr. 1, 1991
4th	Aug. 22, 1997	Feb. 1, 1997	Feb. 1, 1997	Dec. 15, 1994	Mar. 8, 1986

EXAMPLE: *Maribel is from Mexico and is married to a green card holder. Her husband filed an immigration petition for her, and her priority date is February 18, 2004. It is June 10, 2008, and Maribel wants to know if she can apply for a green card yet.*

Maribel would be immigrating in the 2A category since she is the spouse of a green card holder. If you look at the June 2008 visa bulletin, you will see that the 2A category for Mexico has a priority date of May 1, 2002. Thus, people with a priority date of May 1, 2002, or before now can apply for their green cards. Maribel is not yet eligible. It may be several more years before she can apply for her green card.

How do I find out if my priority date is on the visa bulletin?

You can find current dates on the visa bulletin on the Internet by going to http://travel.state.gov/visa/frvi/bulletin/bulletin_1360.html or by calling (202) 663-1541 and listening to a message recorded in English.

Why do people from some countries have to wait so long to get a green card?

Some countries have earlier priority dates, resulting in a longer waiting list, because the law says that only a certain number of preference visas may be issued per country each year. Because the United States annually limits the number of people who can enter and become lawful permanent residents, there is a long line of people waiting to come here. These "per country limits" are the cause of long delays for people from certain countries including Mexico, the Philippines, India, and China. Your wait could be between one and twelve years, or even longer, depending on what country you are from and the preference category in which you fit. And processing delays could increase your waiting time even more.

Under current law, only 480,000 visas may be issued annually for family-based petitions. Of those 480,000 visas, there are no limits on the number of visas that can be issued to immediate relatives, so they account for a large number of the visas used. However, the law says that at least 226,000 visas must be for family-based petitions for family members that are not immediate relatives. Of those 226,000 visas, only 7 percent can go to a specific country.

EXAMPLE: *In any given year, there is often a total of 226,000 visas available for people wanting to immigrate to the United States with family-based petitions. An additional 140,000 visas are available for those with employment-based petitions. Of the 366,000 total visas available worldwide, only 25,620 (7 percent) can go to any specific country. Some countries—like Mexico or the Philippines—typically have many more people eligible for* *the visa than their country's limits. This creates a backlog of people waiting to get a visa.*

Of the 226,000 visas available for those in the preference categories, there is also a limit of the number of visas per preference category. About 10 percent of them are for those in the first preference; about 51 percent are for those in the second preference; about 10 percent are for those in the third preference; and about 29 percent are for those in the fourth preference.

Finally, even when a visa becomes available, there can be processing or other problems at the consulate or the CIS office that account for further delays.

How do I help a family member apply for a green card?

Once the visa petition is approved and when the "priority date" is current, you, as the noncitizen family member, may apply for a green card based on the visa petition. You have to demonstrate not only your relationship to the person filing the petition, but also that you are admissible into the United States. If the government finds that you are inadmissible, the authorities could not only deny your green card application, but also deport you. It is important to see an experienced immigration lawyer or accredited representative to deal with the green card process, most especially inadmissibility and waiver issues.

EXAMPLE: *Susana, a U.S. citizen, filed a family-based petition with an adjustment application (the application for a green card) for her husband, Juan, who entered the country legally but overstayed his visa. Because Juan has been convicted of two fraud crimes, he is inadmissible. However, there is a waiver for this ground of inadmissibility, which Juan files. The CIS* *takes the waiver and tells Juan and Susana that they will decide whether to grant the waiver. Three months later, the CIS denies the waiver. Therefore, CIS will deny Juan's immigration application, and may place Juan in removal (deportation) proceedings.*

If I get a green card through a family member, can my spouse and children immigrate with me?

Probably yes. If you immigrate to the United States through a family member, you will probably be able to bring with you your spouse and unmarried children under the age of twenty-one. However, the procedure is very different for immediate relatives than it is for those who immigrate through the preference categories.

How can I immigrate with my spouse and children if I am an immediate relative?

If you are an immediate relative, you cannot automatically bring your spouse and children with you. But they should be able to immigrate at the same time as you if your U.S. citizen family member directly petitions for them.

> **EXAMPLE:** *Because Olaya is the spouse of Jack, a U.S. citizen, she is an immediate relative. She would like to immigrate to the United States through Jack, bringing with her her daughter Charlotte, who is seven years old and from a previous marriage. Because Olaya and Jack married before Charlotte turned eighteen, Charlotte is Jack's stepdaughter for immigration purposes. Therefore, Jack can file a petition for Charlotte as an immediate relative (the child of a U.S. citizen) as well as for his spouse, Olaya.*

How can I immigrate with my spouse and children if I am immigrating through the preference categories?

If you are immigrating through the preference categories, your spouse and children can be included in your petition and may get their green cards at the same time as you do. In order for them to qualify, your spouse must still be married to you and your children must still be unmarried and under twenty-one at the time you get your green card. Some children over the age of twenty-one may still qualify under something called the Child Status Protection Act, discussed next.

The wait to apply for a green card for some is so long that I fear that even if I petition now for my children, they will be over twenty-one when they are eligible for a green card. What happens then?

A law called the Child Status Protection Act allows some people to apply for a green card as a "child" even after they have turned twenty-one. Because this law is very complicated, you should contact an experienced immigration lawyer or accredited representative if you are facing this situation.

FRAUD ALERT: Beware of anyone who says that they can get you a green card very quickly. Such a person may be a fraud.

What kinds of problems could prevent me from getting a green card and make me inadmissible?

Immigration law includes a list of reasons that would prevent a person from being admitted to the United States and getting a green card, legally called the "grounds of inadmissibility." If you have any of the problems listed below, seek the help of an experienced immigration lawyer or accredited representative before starting the process of obtaining a green card. The grounds-of-inadmissibility list includes:

- Having certain communicable diseases, including active tuberculosis, HIV, gonorrhea, syphilis.
- Not having the proper vaccinations.
- Having a mental or physical disorder that poses a danger to yourself or others (this can include alcoholism).
- Being a drug addict or drug abuser.
- Helping others to enter the United States illegally (also called "alien smuggling").
- Lying or committing fraud to get an immigration benefit such as a visa, entry to the United States, or a green card.
- Lying by claiming to be a U.S. citizen.
- Looking likely to be dependent on cash welfare or long-term care at the government's expense (being a "public charge").
- Posing a threat to national security (for example, spies, terrorists, Nazis, and others).
- Being a draft dodger or draft deserter.
- Voting unlawfully.
- Being a stowaway.
- Coming to the United States to practice polygamy.
- Entering the United States without permission.
- Being in the United States without permission.
- Leaving the United States and then reentering or applying to reenter legally after living in the United States without permission.
- Having a previous deportation or removal order.
- Having a criminal conviction for certain kinds of crimes or

admitting to committing certain kinds of crimes (this includes crimes like assault with a deadly weapon, rape, fraud, arson, murder, and some other less serious crimes).

- Having anything in your past that would give immigration a reason to believe you've been involved in selling drugs.

WARNING: Before starting the green card application process, you should meet with an experienced immigration lawyer or accredited representative to see if any of the grounds of inadmissibility might apply to you.

How will CIS know if I have any of these problems or if I have a criminal record?

Many immigration applications require you to have your fingerprints taken so CIS can perform a criminal background check on you. If you obtain a copy of your FBI report, you will see some of the information CIS will receive from your fingerprints. You may request a copy only of your own FBI background check, not that of someone else.

To request your FBI background check, send a letter asking for a personal review of your FBI background check and include your mailing address (or that of a friend or someone else who can receive mail for you), a copy of your ten fingerprints, and a money order or certified check for $18 payable to "Treasury of the United States" to FBI CIS Division—Record Request, 1000 Custer Hollow Road, Clarksburg, VA 26306. Expect about an eight-to-ten-week wait before you receive a response. If you are on a deadline and need your background check faster, mention that fact in your letter and on the envelope.

If one or more of these grounds of inadmissibility applies to me, is there anything I can do?

In some cases you may be able to obtain a waiver, which is a form of forgiveness from the government, for some of the grounds of inadmissibility. It is essentially as if CIS were saying, "Even though we could deny your entry to the United States, you have shown that you deserve to be admitted and we have decided to let you immigrate." Not all grounds of inadmissibility can be waived. If you need to apply for a waiver, you should consult an experienced immigration lawyer or accredited representative for help. Many of the waivers require that the applicant show that his or her U.S. citizen or legal resident parent or spouse would suffer extreme hardship if the applicant were to be deported to his or her home country.

> **EXAMPLE:** *Gloria is applying for her green card. Five years ago she was convicted of prostitution. The immigration law says that Gloria is inadmissible because she committed prostitution within the last ten years. Gloria is lucky that there is a waiver available. If the CIS grants the waiver, it will have waived or pardoned her crime. Then Gloria's application can be approved. If the CIS denies the waiver, it will deny her green card application and may deport her.*

> **EXAMPLE:** *Juan is applying for his green card through his U.S. citizen wife. Someone helped them fill out the forms, but that person did not know immigration law. The last time Juan entered the United States with his tourist visa in 1996, he lied to the immigra-*

tion officer, telling him that he was coming for a short visit. In reality he was returning to resume his residence of five years in the United States. This act makes him inadmissible because of a material misrepresentation. A material misrepresentation is one that could have made a difference in the immigration officer's decision as to whether Juan should have been allowed to enter. It was material in this case because if Juan had told the officer the truth, the officer would not have let him return to the United States since Juan's purpose was not to visit. There is a waiver available for Juan if he can show that his wife would suffer extreme hardship if Juan is denied his green card. If the CIS denies Juan's waiver request, his green card application will be denied, and if Juan is in the United States, there is a chance that he will be deported.

Where will I have to go for my green card interview?

Your green card interview may take place either in the United States or at a U.S. consulate in your home country. If you are already living in the United States and are eligible to have your green card interview here, you will go through adjustment of status (discussed on page 43) in the United States. Not everyone who is here is eligible to do this. However, if you are, it is helpful because it means you can stay in the United States during the process, and if you are denied, it is still possible to find a way to stay in the country.

If you currently are living abroad, you will go through consular processing. You thus would submit your application and be interviewed at a U.S. consulate in your home country.

EXAMPLE: *Bernardo is in the United States on a student visa. His wife, Cynthia, is a U.S. citizen who files a family-based petition for Bernardo. He will not have to leave the United States to get his green card and can have his interview at the local CIS office.*

EXAMPLE: *Carlos is a lawful permanent resident who filed a family-based petition for his wife, Andrea, who lives in Guadalajara, Mexico. She is waiting for her priority date under the 2A preference category to be current on the State Department visa bulletin. When it is current, she will have her green card interview at the U.S. consulate in Ciudad Juarez.*

What are the requirements for me to stay in the United States to get my green card (adjustment of status)?

In order to qualify for adjustment of status, and have your green card interview in the United States, you must be living in the United States and meet one of the following requirements.

1. You entered the country legally (that is, with the permission of the immigration authorities) and are still living here legally; OR
2. You entered the United States legally, and regardless of whether you are still living here legally, you fit in the immediate relative category; OR
3. You entered illegally or are no longer legally here in the United States and a relative filed a visa petition for you by April 30, 2001. There are additional requirements for those whose visa petition was filed after January 14, 1998, and on or before April 30, 2001. Except for a few situations, you must pay an additional $1,000 penalty fee if you fall under this category, which was created by the law called Section 245(i). You should consult an experienced immigration lawyer or accredited representative if you think you might qualify under this section.

EXAMPLE: *Elizabeth entered the United States on a tourist visa from Peru. Her visa expired in 2003, but she remained in the* *country. She is now married to a U.S. citizen but is undocumented. She will be able to have her green card interview in the United States because she originally entered the country with permission AND, as the spouse of a U.S. citizen, is an immediate relative.*

EXAMPLE: *Armando crossed the border without permission in 1994 and has been in the United States without papers ever since. In 1999, he married his wife, who is a green card holder and filed a family-based petition for him in July 1999. When Armando applies for his green card, he will be able to file it in the United States and have his interview here because he qualifies under Section 245(i). He will need to pay a $1,000 penalty fee to qualify for this benefit.*

What if I am in the United States with an approved family petition, but I do not qualify to have my green card interview here? What happens to me then?

If you do not qualify to stay in the United States to have your green card interview, you must return to your home country to process your application. There are potentially great risks in doing this if you are undocumented because you may face the unlawful presence bars upon leaving the United States, even if you have an approved family-based petition or other basis for getting a green card.

EXAMPLE: *Saul came to the United States from Mexico on a student visa. Once his visa expired, he decided to stay here and has been undocumented for three years. Earlier this year he married a green card holder in the United States. His wife can file a family-based petition for Saul. However, when he is eligible to apply for a green card, he will have to apply through the U.S. consulate in Mexico because, although he originally entered the United States* *legally, he is not an immediate relative. He also does not qualify for Section 245(i) because his wife did not file her petition for him by April 30, 2001. Therefore, he will need to go to Mexico for his green card interview and will be subject to the unlawful presence bar. He will be barred from returning to the United States for ten years unless he can qualify for a waiver (see page 41 and next question below). For that reason, Saul may decide to wait until his wife becomes a U.S. citizen, which would allow him to adjust his status and therefore not be subject to the ten-year bar.*

I am in the United States, but I have no papers. What are the risks for me if I leave the country to have my green card interview?

If you are in the United States without papers and you leave the country, you may be barred from returning here for up to ten years. This is the case even if you leave only to attend a green card interview. If you also reenter or try to reenter the United States without permission, you may be barred from returning here permanently. Make sure to consult an experienced immigration lawyer or an accredited representative before voluntarily leaving the United States if you've been here without papers for more than 180 days.

How do I figure out which forms I need to submit to get my green card in the United States (adjustment of status)?

Because forms sometimes change, you should check on the CIS Web site (www.uscis.gov) to make sure you have the most current forms to submit.

Where can I get the immigration forms I need?

There are four ways to obtain for free the immigration forms you need from CIS.

First, you can go to any local CIS office and pick up immigration forms. However, you may have to wait in line a long time. If you are undocumented, you also may expose yourself to immigration authorities, which is risky.

Second, you can order immigration forms from CIS on the phone. The toll-free number is (800) 870-3676. This service is available in English and Spanish. Once the automated message starts, press 2 to hear the message in Spanish.

Third, you can download the forms directly from the CIS Web site at www.uscis.gov. Click on "Forms." If you can't download and print forms from your computer, the CIS Web site also allows you to order forms to be sent to you. Look for a place to click on "Forms by Mail."

Finally, if a lawyer or accredited representative is helping you with your case, he or she should be able to provide you with the immigration forms. The lawyer or accredited representative should not charge you just to give you the forms, as they are available for free.

Where do I send my completed green card application for adjustment of status?

The exact mailing address is available on the CIS Web site. The filing location may change, so you should always check the CIS Web site before submitting any form.

> **WARNING:** Whenever you send immigration forms to CIS, always send them certified mail, return receipt requested, so you will have proof that you submitted your forms.
>
>   Also, ALWAYS KEEP A COPY OF EVERYTHING YOU SEND TO CIS. Your lawyer, accredited representative, CIS, or the mail service may lose your documents. It is helpful to keep a copy in case you need to file your forms again or if you later need proof of CIS notices you receive.

How much will it cost for me to file my green card application?

The cost for a green card application (not including the family-based petition from step one) in 2008 ranges from $600 to over $2,000 for all of the filing fees. Fees vary depending on which forms you are submitting, how old you are, whether you have to pay the $1,000 penalty because you qualify by means of Section 245(i), and whether you need a waiver. Filing fees also change frequently and the amount printed on an immigration form may be wrong. You should always consult the CIS Web site at www.uscis .gov for the most current filing fee information.

WARNING: Your application may be delayed or returned if you do not submit the correct filing fee amount, so be careful to make sure you are submitting the correct filing fee.

How do I schedule a medical exam for my green card application?

You must go to a CIS-certified doctor to have your green card medical exam done, and the results of the exam must be included on Form I-693. To find a CIS-certified doctor in your area, call the CIS National Customer Service Center at (800) 375-5283. The information on this toll-free number is available in Spanish. You can also find information on CIS-certified doctors in your area on the CIS Web site at http://www.uscis.gov/graphics/exec/cs/index.asp.

How can I check the status of my case?

The best way to check the status of your case is either by making an InfoPass appointment with the CIS or contacting CIS. You can also go on their Web site to check the status of your case. To make an InfoPass appointment for a meeting at the local CIS office, go to the CIS Web site at http://infopass.uscis.gov. To contact CIS by telephone, call the National Customer Service Center at (800) 375-5283. You also can check the status of your pending application on the Internet by visiting the CIS Web site at www.uscis.gov and clicking on "Case Status & Processing Dates."

What will happen at my green card/adjustment-of-status interview?

After you have properly submitted all of your immigration applications, you will receive a notice to have your fingerprints taken, and then later another notice to come in for your green card interview. Because the CIS officer during your green card interview will review the information in the forms you submitted, you should keep copies of everything you submitted and review this material before the interview. The examiner will check to make sure that the petition your family member filed for you is still valid and determine if the required family relationship exists. (This is usually a problem only if your spouse petitioned for you and you are now divorced or your petitioner has died.) If your spouse petitioned for you, the examiner will verify that you have a real marriage and not one entered into for a green card.

During your interview, the CIS officer will check closely to see if any of the inadmissibility grounds apply to you. It is important

WARNING: TRAVELING TO YOUR HOME COUNTRY BEFORE YOUR GREEN CARD INTERVIEW

CIS may grant permission for you to leave the United States for a short period of time once you have submitted your green card application. This permission is called advance parole. It requires a separate application. However, you may face serious risks if you leave the country. Even if the CIS authorizes your trip abroad, if you leave the United States you could destroy your chance of getting a green card. Be sure to consult an experienced immigration lawyer or accredited representative *before* leaving the country with advance parole.

that you can prove that you are admissible, that is, you do not have any of the problems listed on the "grounds of inadmissibility" discussed earlier in this chapter (see page 39). If any of the grounds of inadmissibility apply to you, you will have to apply for a waiver, assuming that one is available. If you are ineligible for a waiver or you apply for one but CIS denies it, your green card application will be denied, and you might be placed in removal (deportation) proceedings.

EXAMPLE: *Rosa is eligible to apply for a green card, so she goes to a CIS-certified doctor to undergo the medical exam that is required as part of her application. The doctor notes that Rosa has infectious syphilis, a disease on the "grounds of inadmissibility" list. The CIS officer will know about Rosa's infectious syphilis at the interview because Rosa must bring a copy of her medical exam. Fortunately, there is a waiver available to Rosa because she is the spouse of a green card holder.*

EXAMPLE: *Enrique is applying for a green card through his U.S. citizen brother. He originally entered the United States in 2000 by telling the border patrol agent he was a U.S. citizen and showing his brother's U.S. passport. He then applied for a driver's license using his brother's U.S. birth certificate. The CIS officer at his green card interview might find out about these things either through the government's computer system or by asking Enrique directly if he has ever said he was a U.S. citizen to enter the country. Because Enrique lied when he indicated he was a U.S. citizen, he will be barred from getting a green card and may be deported. Unfortunately, there is no waiver available for him.*

If my green card interview goes well, will I get my green card/adjustment of status right away?

If CIS approves your application at your interview, they will mail your green card to you rather than give it to you at the interview. You should receive your green card in a few weeks. Make sure CIS has your current and correct address!

What is the process for getting my green card through a U.S. consulate (consular processing)?

Under the consular processing system, CIS will forward your file to the U.S. consulate in your home country that processes green cards. Not all U.S. consulates abroad process green card applications. For example, while there are several U.S. consulates in Mexico, only Ciudad Juarez processes green cards.

CIS first completes processing the visa petition, and receives the affidavit of support and other information that it has requested of your family member who filed the petition for you. The DOS then takes over your application.

The U.S. consulate (part of DOS) will send you a packet of

forms to complete when your turn comes up on the waiting list. This packet includes many important documents, including a notice telling you when and where your green card interview will take place, as well as information about where you have to go for a medical exam and additional forms you must complete.

What will happen at my green card interview for consular processing?

A green card interview at a U.S. consulate covers many of the same issues described in the discussion of the adjustment-of-status green card interview. During your interview, the examiner seeks to answer the following:

- Are you who you claim to be?
- Are you really related to the person who filed the petition, and do the two of you still have the required relationship?
- Do you fall within any of the grounds of inadmissibility mentioned above? If so, are you eligible for a waiver?

One very common ground of inadmissibility that people face in consular processing is the unlawful presence bars, described in chapter 1. A waiver is available for three- and ten-year bars, but

---

WARNING: CONSULT AN EXPERIENCED IMMIGRATION LAWYER OR ACCREDITED REPRESENTATIVE BEFORE CONSULAR PROCESSING

If you are currently in the United States, it is especially important to obtain legal advice before going through consular processing because you may be unable to return to the United States if your green card application is denied.

it's essential to obtain legal advice from an experienced immigration lawyer or accredited representative who is familiar with your U.S. consulate's decisions on waiver applications.

> **EXAMPLE:** *Jaime entered the United States without permission three years ago from Mexico. He married Susanna, a U.S. citizen. Susanna has filed a visa petition for Jaime, and the petition has been approved. Jaime and Susanna now have to make a very difficult decision. The only way Jaime can immigrate is by having his green card interview at the U.S. consulate in Ciudad Juarez, Mexico. He cannot process his green card application in the United States because he did not enter with permission. Yet the act of leaving the United States could mean that Jaime will be unable to return for ten years. However, there is a waiver available. Although the U.S. consulate and CIS officers in Ciudad Juarez have been approving the majority of these waivers in cases represented by a lawyer, lately there has been an increase in denials.*
>
> *Jaime and Susan decide to risk leaving the United States for the interview at Ciudad Juarez. Jaime goes to the appointment there, taking with him a detailed waiver application prepared by his lawyer or accredited representative that describes the extreme hardship that Susanna would suffer if Jaime were not permitted to immigrate. The application and the waiver are forwarded to a CIS officer in Mexico. During the time it takes CIS to make a decision on Jaime's waiver request, he must remain outside the United States; this can range anywhere from four to ten months or even longer.*
>
> *The CIS approves Jamie's waiver application. He returns to the consulate, where he is issued an immigrant visa. Jaime becomes a lawful permanent resident as soon as he enters the United States and the immigration authorities stamp his pass-*

port. Had the CIS denied the waiver, Jaime would have had to stay in Mexico for ten years. Please note that aside from the U.S. consulate in Ciudad Juarez, many other U.S. consulates deny a high percentage of these waiver applications. It is thus vitally important that you consult with an experienced immigration lawyer or accredited representative before leaving the United States.

If my green card/consular processing interview goes well, will I get my green card right away?

If your application is approved at your consular processing interview, the consular officer will give you some papers (including an immigrant visa) in a sealed envelope to show at the U.S. border, where you will apply for admission. At the border, Customs and Border Protection (CBP) will stamp your passport and you will be a permanent resident as of the day you enter the country. You will receive your green card in the mail within a few months. Please make sure the authorities have your correct mailing address.

What is an affidavit of support?

All green card applicants who are petitioned by a family member must submit an affidavit of support on Form I-864 with their green card application. The purpose of the affidavit of support is to show that you are unlikely to be a public charge, that is, it is unlikely you will live off of government benefits such as welfare or food stamps. Your family member who petitioned for you must be your sponsor and submit the affidavit of support for you that lists your sponsor's income. In order for you to get your green card, your sponsor's total income must be 125 percent of the poverty level for a family that includes all members of your sponsor's immediate family members living with her/him, as well as all the people who are applying for a green card.

> **EXAMPLE:** *Juan is applying for his green card through a petition filed by his U.S. citizen father, Marcos. Juan's wife and child are also applying to immigrate. Marcos lives with his wife and one child, who is still in school. So the total number of family members that are counted is six (that includes three from Juan's family and three from Marcos's family). Marcos's wife also works. Their combined annual income is $40,000 a year. In 2008, 125 percent of the poverty guidelines for a family of six was $35,500. Since the sponsors' income is greater than the poverty guidelines amount, Marco meets the affidavit-of-support requirement for Juan and his family to get green cards.*

WHERE TO FIND THE CURRENT FEDERAL POVERTY GUIDELINES

The easiest way is to check the CIS Web site, at http://www.uscis .gov. These guidelines change annually. Below are the minimum income requirements in 2008 to sponsor a family member:

Sponsor's Household Size	125% of poverty guidelines
2	$17,500
3	$22,000
4	$26,500
5	$31,000
6	$35,500
7	$40,000
8	$44,500

The amounts are lower for some sponsors on active duty in the U.S. armed forces and higher for sponsors living in Alaska and Hawaii.

What if my sponsor's total income is less than the amount required?

If the family member who petitioned for you has an insufficient income to sponsor you given affidavit-of-support requirements, a different person (for example a friend or another relative) who must be a U.S. citizen or lawful permanent resident living in the United States may also be your sponsor on a separate affidavit of support. The other sponsor's income must be greater than the income requirement. The incomes of the two affidavits cannot be combined to meet the requirement.

What is the significance of an affidavit of support for my sponsor?

The affidavit of support that is required in family immigration cases is enforceable. This means that the affidavit is a binding contract for your sponsor to support you. Your sponsor may be responsible to repay certain public benefits, if you receive them. So far, there have not been many cases in which a sponsor has had to repay the government for public benefits an immigrating family member receives, except in the case where a person petitions for his spouse and the marriage later ends. However, the affidavit of support is legally binding and could be enforced.

When does the sponsor's responsibility end?

A sponsor who signs an affidavit of support is not responsible for public benefits such as welfare or food stamps used by the immigrating family member after he/she:

- Becomes a U.S. citizen;
- Earns credit for forty quarters (about ten years) of work history in the United States according to the Social Security Administration, either through his or her own work or a spouse's or parent's work; or
- Dies.

3

Getting Help from
Your Employer

There are several different kinds of work-related, nonimmigrant visas. These visas give people the right to enter and remain in the United States temporarily for a specific purpose. While many are temporary, others can lead to a green card.

What are temporary work visas called and who are they for?

There are a number of different temporary work visas, all discussed in this chapter. The most common ones are:

- H-1B visa for professionals in specialty occupations;
- H-2A visa for seasonal agricultural workers;
- H-2B visa for seasonal nonagricultural workers; and
- TN visas for people from Canada and Mexico in certain occupations.

Temporary H visas allow immigrants to remain in the United States for a set period of time and work legally for the employer who petitions for them. If they want to get a new job, they may need to get a new visa.

The H visas allow workers to travel in and out of the United States and, in some cases, bring along certain family members. The family members who come to the country with the H visa holder cannot work legally here.

APPLYING FOR H VISAS

Each H visa has different requirements and different benefits.

- **The H-1B visa** requires a sponsoring U.S. employer. The employer must first file an application with the Department of Labor (DOL), called a Labor Condition Application (LCA), confirming the working conditions offered and that the employer will pay the prevailing wages (the average wage for that job in that particular part of the country). Once the DOL certifies the application, the employer then files a petition for the worker with Citizenship and Immigration Services (CIS). If CIS approves the petition, the worker may apply for the H-1B visa, admission to the United States, or a change of status if already in the United States on another type of visa.

    Under current law, H-1B status is granted initially for up to three years and lasts for a maximum period of six years. After the six-year period, the immigrant must remain outside the United States for one year before another H-1B petition can be approved. Under certain circumstances, immigrants may be granted an extension of H-1B status beyond the six-year maximum period if they are in the process of getting a green card through their employment.

    H-1B visa holders may adjust their status if they have a

valid approved immigrant visa (either through their employment or family relationship).

- **The H-2A visa** is available for temporary seasonal agricultural workers who are sponsored by an employer after the employer has attempted to, but cannot, find U.S workers to fill the jobs.

  Temporary seasonal work is work performed during certain seasons of the year—for example, harvesting a crop—or for a period of less than a year when the employer can show that the need for workers is temporary.

  The H-2A visa lasts only as long as the job lasts. It can be issued for a period of up to 364 days. The visa can be renewed each year for up to three years total.

  The employer must show that there are not enough able, willing, and qualified U.S. workers available to do the work at the time and place needed. This means that the employer must first attempt to recruit workers throughout a multistate region of his or her part of the country. If the employer cannot find workers in the United States to do the job, he or she may recruit crews of temporary workers from abroad.

  The employer also must show that hiring immigrant workers will not have an adverse effect on the wages or working conditions of U.S. workers. Finally, employers are required to provide H-2A workers with certain benefits:

  —transportation home or to the next workplace when the contract period is up;
  —transportation to and from the worker's temporary home to the workplace;
  —housing to all workers who do not commute—the housing must meet minimum federal standards for temporary labor camps;

— three meals a day or facilities in which the worker can prepare food;

— tools and supplies necessary to perform the work; and

— workers' compensation insurance.

If your employer isn't offering these benefits, you should
seek advice from an experienced immigration lawyer or accredited representative. You also could consult with local
community and religious leaders that you know. You also can
complain directly to the DOL. The employer should have
given you a copy of your file and application that includes a
number you can call at DOL to complain if you are not provided these benefits.

- **The H-2B visa** is for temporary workers to work on nonagricultural seasonal or intermittent work or on jobs necessary
because of a onetime occurrence. Typically, H-2B workers fill
jobs in the service sector in areas including construction,
health care, landscaping, lumber, manufacturing, and food
service/processing. The most important part about the job is
not what kind of work it involves, but that it is temporary.

  Under current law, the H-2B visa does not offer a path to
permanent residency. Congress has been debating bills that
would offer a path to permanent residency for H-2B workers.
However, no such bill has become law.

  The H-2B visa lasts only as long as the job lasts. While this
visa can be issued for a period of up to one year, the Department of Labor doesn't issue this kind of visa for more than
nine months. However, this visa can be renewed each year for
up to three years total.

- **The TN visa, or Trade NAFTA visa,** was created by the North
American Free Trade Agreement of 1994. It is a visa category

established for Canadian and Mexican professionals to live and work temporarily in the United States. Only certain occupations qualify a worker for the TN visa. TN visa holders can bring their spouses and unmarried children to the United States, but these spouses and children will not have permission to work here.

The only occupations that qualify for the TN visa are those included on the NAFTA Professional Job Series List that can be found on the State Department Web site at http://travel.state.gov/visa/temp/types/types_1274.html. With some exceptions, each profession requires a baccalaureate degree for an entry-level job. The list comprises more than seventy professions, including accountants, librarians, medical professionals, scientists, graphic designers, teachers, and social workers.

Application procedures are different for Canadians and Mexicans. This book focuses on the procedures for Mexican nationals who may apply at U.S. embassies and consulates around the world.

To apply for a TN visa, you must submit a visa application form to a U.S. consular office (anywhere in the world but preferably in Mexico) with a letter of employment for a job in the United States. The letter must indicate that the job requires your employment in a professional capacity. You must present evidence that you have the necessary credentials for that profession. As part of the visa application process, like most visa applicants, you must be interviewed at the embassy's consular section. Interviews generally are by appointment only. As part of the visa interview, a quick, two-digit, ink-free fingerprint scan will usually be taken.

Like most applicants, you can expect to wait for an interview appointment for a few weeks or less. However, you can expect to wait considerably longer for some embassy consular sections. Visa wait times for interview appointments and visa processing time information for each U.S. embassy or consulate worldwide is now available on the State Department Web site (at http://travel.state.gov/visa/temp/wait/tempvisitors_wait.php at Visa Wait Times) and on most embassy Web sites. Visit the Embassy Consular Section Web site where you will apply for your visa to find out how to schedule an interview appointment, pay the fees, and any other instructions. Among other things, you will be required to submit some government forms, pay certain fees, and have a passport valid for travel to the United States, a photograph, and a letter of employment. Because procedures differ by county, you should consult the Department of State Web site at http://travel.state.gov/visa/temp/types/types_1274.html to make sure you have accurate information and the appropriate materials.

GETTING A GREEN CARD THROUGH WORK

The U.S. government annually issues 140,000 "employment based" permanent visas largely to people who are sponsored by their employers and have permanent offers of employment here. People with these employment-based visas are eligible to receive green cards. Employment-based immigration (like family-based immigration) is based on a "preference system" with different categories of workers and different wait times. Some people who are eligible through their work also must have a "labor certification" proving that they are not taking a job that a U.S. worker could fill.

What is labor certification?

A labor certification is a certificate, issued by the DOL, that says there is a shortage of U.S. workers for a certain job and the person for whom the application for a labor certification was filed is qualified to perform the job. A labor certification does not give employment authorization, but obtaining one is usually the first step toward obtaining lawful permanent residence through employment. In 2007, in order to reduce incentives and opportunities to commit fraud and abuse in the labor certification process, the U.S. Department of Labor, Employment and Training Administration issued regulations altering the labor certification program. Among other things, these new regulations:

- Prohibit the substitution of an alien beneficiary on any application for permanent labor certification;
- Prohibit the sale, barter, or purchase of a permanent labor certification or approved labor certification;
- Prohibit an employer from seeking or receiving payment of any kind for any activity related to obtaining a permanent labor certification. ("Payment" includes deduction from wages or benefits);
- Require that all costs related to preparing, filing, and/or obtaining a permanent labor certification be borne by the employer. The alien beneficiary is prohibited from paying for any activity related to obtaining a permanent labor certification. This includes attorney fees and fees associated with recruitment activity;
- Established an expiration date of an approved permanent labor certification. A permanent labor certification will expire 180 days from the date of issue.

This is a long and complicated process. An application for a labor certification is filed by a U.S. employer on behalf of an immigrant who has the skills necessary for the job the employer wishes to fill. The employer must prove that there is a shortage of

U.S. workers for the job, that the person for whom the application is filed has the necessary skills to do the job, and that the employer will pay the employee the proper wage before the DOL will issue the labor certification.

Getting a labor certification can be difficult because of the presumption under American immigration law that American workers can fill most jobs in the United States and that new immigrants are thus not needed. Immigrants for EB-2 and EB-3 visas, discussed in detail in the next section, must prove that *the particular job being offered to them* is an exception to this presumption and that their skills are in short supply here by showing that U.S. workers either do not have the skills or training to perform the job or do not want the jobs at the pay offered. Workers seeking EB-2 and EB-3 visas also must prove that they have the necessary job experience. In addition, the particular job being offered must be both permanent and full-time and the employer must be willing and able to pay the worker the average wage in the location in which the job is being offered.

Your prospective employer first must try, and fail, to recruit potential U.S. job applicants and thereby demonstrate a shortage of workers qualified for the job in the geographic location. The employer then files labor certification papers with the DOL to prove that no American workers are willing or able to take the particular job offered to you. If the labor certification is approved, the date the labor certification is filed becomes your priority date for adjustment purposes.

FRAUD WARNING: Beware of anyone who says that he or she can easily and quickly get you a labor certification. Such a person may be a fraud, and this is a common scam.

As the sponsored worker in the labor certification process, you are completely dependent on your potential employer because the employer, not you the immigrant, must file the application and the employer can withdraw the application at any time.

Once the DOL approves your labor certification, your employer must file a visa petition (form I-140) with CIS and attach the labor certification to it. This is the second step in becoming a permanent resident through employment. In addition to the labor certification, you also must submit letters of reference and other evidence proving your relevant job experience.

EMPLOYMENT-BASED VISAS

Here's a look at employment-based visas:

- **EB-1** includes people with extraordinary abilities who are at the very top of their professions (including athletes, artists, scientists, and others who are internationally recognized), outstanding professors and researchers, and executives and managers of multinational companies. Not very many people qualify for this type of visa. People who qualify are not required to submit a labor certification and can immigrate relatively easily.

- **EB-2** includes professionals with advanced degrees (a master's degree or higher or a bachelor's degree and at least five years of professional experience) and people with exceptional ability. These workers generally must have a labor certification and a permanent full-time job offer. However, some EB-2 workers do not need a job offer or a labor certification if they can show that their immigration would be in the "national interest" of the United States. While it is difficult to show that a person's immigration would be in this country's national interest, some of the factors that are considered include whether the work will improve the U.S. economy or the wages and working conditions of U.S. workers, the work will improve the environment or make better use of natural resources, or the work will improve education, health care, or housing for the underprivileged.

- **EB-3** includes professionals with bachelor's degrees, skilled workers, and unskilled workers. All workers in this category must have a permanent full-time job offer in the United States. The employer, not the immigrant, must file the immigration petition. Other than professional nurses and licensed physical therapists, everyone in this category must have a labor certification. A skilled occupation requires at least two years of experience and includes such jobs as bakers, welders, inspectors, and paralegals. Unskilled jobs, defined as jobs that can be learned in less than two years, include bartenders and typists. It can be very difficult to obtain a visa for unskilled work because it is hard to show that there are no American workers who can do these jobs.

- **EB-4** includes ten different categories of workers, the best known being religious workers. Religious workers do not have to show a labor certification and generally do not have to wait long to get a visa. However, they must show that they have a job offer in the United States. Religious workers include ordained or authorized ministers, religious professionals (including teachers and others who have a bachelor's degree), and religious vocational and occupational workers (including monks, nuns, and religious counselors). Other people who work for religious organizations but don't have specialized religious training, such as janitors, maintenance workers, fund-raisers, and administrative workers, do not qualify for a religious visa.

Priority Dates

Employment-based category	All countries except China, India, Mexico, and the Philippines	China–mainland	India	Mexico	Philippines
1st	Current	Current	Current	Current	Current
2nd	Current	Apr. 22, 2005	Jan. 8, 2003	Current	Current
3rd	Aug. 1, 2002	Aug. 1, 2002	Apr. 22, 2001	May 8, 2001	Aug. 1, 2002
Schedule A Workers	Unavailable	Unavailable	Unavailable	Unavailable	Unavailable
Other Workers	Oct. 1, 2001	Oct. 1, 2001	Oct. 1, 2001	Oct. 1, 2001	Oct. 1, 2001
4th	Current	Current	Current	Current	Current
Certain Religious Workers	Current	Current	Current	Current	Current
Iraqi & Afghani Translators	Sept. 18, 2006	Sept. 18, 2006	Sept. 18, 2006	Sept. 18, 2006	Sept. 18, 2006
5th	Current	Current	Current	Current	Current
Targeted Employment Areas/ Regional Centers	Current	Current	Current	Current	Current

- **EB-5** often is called the "millionaire's visa" because eligible people must be able to invest $1 million (or $500,000 under certain circumstances) in the United States and manage a business that will create at least ten full-time jobs. This visa was intended to encourage new investment in the United States and the creation of new jobs. Those eligible for this category do not need to have a labor certification or a permanent job offer.

IF YOUR VISA PETITION IS APPROVED

If the visa petition filed by the employer is approved, and your priority date is current, you can file an application for adjustment of status or for consular processing, discussed in the previous chapter, depending on which way you will use to immigrate through your employment. (Your priority date is either the date your labor certification is filed or the date your preference petition is filed, depending on your preference category.) This is the third and final step toward immigrating through your employment.

> **WARNING:** Before starting the visa petition process, you should meet with an experienced immigration lawyer or accredited representative to see if any of the grounds of inadmissibility might apply to you.

What could stop me from getting my green card through work?

Immigration law includes a list of reasons that would prevent a person from being admitted to the United States and getting a green card. Just as there are "grounds of inadmissibility" for family-sponsored petitions, there are grounds for employment-based petitions. See the list on pages 39–40 for reasons you might be considered inadmissible, and how you might seek a waiver for certain circumstances.

IF YOUR EMPLOYER CHANGES HIS OR HER MIND

There's not much you can do if your employer changes his or her mind about sponsoring you, no matter how long you've waited. In the current economic climate, employers often change their minds, reorganize, or close down. Most workers with an approved labor certification cannot substitute a new employer for their original sponsoring employer. If your original employer is no longer in business, you must find another employer and go through the labor certification process all over again. However, if you find a new employer, you may be able to keep your original priority date instead of having to wait again to apply for a green card.

What's next? Adjustment of Status

If you have an approved employment-based petition, then, like all applicants for a green card, you must submit all required documents, photographs, immigration forms, applications with the correct fees, medical examination results, fingerprints, and photographs. You also must show that you are not inadmissible. Finally, you may also have to go to an interview.

For employment-based immigrants, the process for getting a green card adjustment of status is usually fairly straightforward. However, processing delays and bureaucratic problems can turn an easy process into a difficult one. Processing times currently range from one to two years, depending on the CIS office that handles and receives the case.

Most employment-based immigrants can get their green cards without even a single interview at the CIS and can also get their green cards even if they have been out of legal immigration status (with section 245(i) protection) or worked previously in the United States. But to do so, they must not have worked without authorization or been out of status for more than 180 days total. It is very important that you check with an experienced immigration lawyer or accredited representative to determine if you qualify for a green card if you have been out of status or worked previously without authorization.

Where do I send my employment-based adjustment-of-status green card application?

Where you send your green card application depends on where you reside or where your employer is located. Please refer to the USCIS Web site (www.uscis.gov) for the appropriate place to send your application (in this case, it would be an Immigration Services center).

Once I get my green card, do I have to work for the same employer who filed my labor certification application?

It is very important for you to work for your sponsoring employer when you get your green card because the immigration petition is based on a permanent job offer that both you and your employer intended to honor. You, like other workers in your situation, put yourself at risk if you never work for your sponsoring employer after getting your green card. However, if the CIS takes more than 180 days to process your application for a green card adjustment of status, then you are not required to work for the sponsoring employer when you finally get your green card. You may obtain a new job, but that job must be in the same or a similar occupation. This provision helps you if you want to pursue a better job opportunity.

4

What You Must Know About Deportation and Detention

You've worked very hard to get the right paperwork in order and the process has probably been long. Your job isn't over yet. Your legal status in the United States won't last forever unless you take steps to keep your status current.

Here's what you need to know to stay legal, and if you run into trouble, here's the information you need to understand what the consequences might be.

What is deportation?

Deportation is the act by which the U.S. government forces someone out of the country because he or she has violated immigration laws. Under current immigration law, this process is called "removal." Someone deported from the United States will be sent back to his or her home country.

WHAT IS ICE?

ICE stands for the Bureau of Immigration and Customs Enforcement. It is the government agency in charge of immigration enforcement inside the U.S.—including deportation and
immigration detention. The Immigration and Naturalization
Service (INS or *la migra*) used to fulfill these functions. The
Department of Homeland Security took over the INS in 2003
and created ICE (for deportation and detention), the Bureau of
Citizenship and Immigration Services (CIS) (for immigration
services like green card, visa and naturalization services) and
the Bureau of Customs and Border Protection (CBP) (for immigration enforcement at the border). The INS no longer exists.

Who is subject to deportation?

It is important to know that undocumented people are not
the only people who can be deported. People with visas and
even green cards who have been in the United States for almost
their entire lives and have U.S. citizen family members also can be
deported. In fact, anyone who is not a U.S. citizen can be
deported.

EXAMPLE: *Arturo came to the United States when he was three
years old and has lived here ever since. He is now fifty-seven years
old and got a green card when he was twenty-three years old
through his U.S. citizen wife. Together they have three children,
all of whom were born in the United States and are U.S. citizens.
Recently, Arturo fired his handgun into the sky to scare off some
drunken neighbors in front of his house. Although his gun was
properly registered, Arturo received a criminal conviction for
unlawful discharge of a firearm. This conviction can make him*

deportable even though he is a longtime permanent resident with U.S. citizen family members.

There are many reasons why people are deported. For example, you could be deportable if you are unlawfully present in the United States, entered the United States without the government's permission, helped to smuggle someone into the country, falsely claimed to be a U.S. citizen, committed marriage fraud, became a public charge, or unlawfully voted. The immigration law includes a more complete list of things that would make you deportable.

Many people with a criminal arrest or conviction also are deportable. For example, you could be deported for the following:

- Almost any drug conviction including even simple possession or a misdemeanor. (You also can be deportable for admitting that you were a drug addict or drug abuser in the past.)
- Theft offenses, depending on your immigration status and the sentence you received.
- Violent crimes such as assault, battery, rape, or murder.
- Domestic violence convictions or convictions for violating an order of protection.
- Any conviction for sex offenses including consensual sex with a minor (someone under the age of eighteen).
- Gun convictions.

There are two different kinds of proceedings that can result in deportation—regular deportation proceedings, now called removal proceedings, and an abbreviated proceeding, often called expedited removal.

> **WARNING:** If you have had *any* contact with the criminal justice system, including any arrests that did not lead to a conviction or even a conviction that might have been erased from your record and happened many years ago, you still need to avoid any contact with immigration authorities until you talk to an experienced immigration lawyer or accredited representative.

REGULAR DEPORTATION/REMOVAL PROCEEDINGS

The first step in the deportation process often is your arrest and detention by ICE. ICE stands for the Bureau of Immigration and Customs Enforcement. It is the government agency in charge of immigration enforcement inside the United States, including deportation and immigration detention.

If you are arrested and detained, ICE may hold you at a private prison, a local county jail, or a federal immigration detention center. You may be detained close to home or very far from home (i.e., outside of the state where you live). ICE must give you a "notice to appear" within seventy-two hours of your arrest. A "notice to appear" is a piece of paper that explains in English why ICE wants to deport you and will indicate where and when to appear for your immigration hearing in front of an immigration judge.

In other cases, you may not be arrested or detained, but are told that you are going to be deported. ICE must make sure that you receive a notice to appear in the mail.

> **WARNING: YOU MUST ATTEND ALL DEPORTATION HEARINGS**
>
> If you miss a deportation hearing, you may be deported even though you were not present and may become ineligible to apply for any immigration benefit for ten years.

If ICE arrests and detains you, you will have a bond hearing, the first hearing in the deportation process. At this hearing, an immigration judge can decide either the amount of money you must pay to be released from immigration detention while your case is pending, or that you cannot be released until your case is finished because of criminal issues in your past. If the judge allows you to be released (bond out), the minimum bond amount currently is $1,500. While you can ask the immigration judge to lower your bond, the judge has complete discretion to determine the amount.

WARNING: FIND AN EXPERIENCED IMMIGRATION LAWYER TO HELP YOU IF YOU ARE IN REMOVAL PROCEEDINGS

If you are in removal proceedings and do not have an attorney, tell the immigration judge that you would like time to find a lawyer. Do not say anything to the judge or ICE about your case, such as admitting that you are deportable, because you might give the government more information against you and ruin your chances to stay in this country.

The next step after the bond hearing is the master calendar hearing, which determines if you are really deportable. The judge may think you are not deportable. Or you may be eligible for an immigration option that would allow you to stay in the United States even if you were deportable. In either of those cases, the judge will schedule another hearing called an individual hearing. At this hearing, you or your lawyer (if you have one) will argue why you are not deportable and/or why you deserve to be able to remain in the United States. At the end of this hearing, the judge will either order you deported or determine that you can stay.

If the judge finds that you are deportable and that you cannot stay in the United States, then he or she will enter an order of deportation against you. If you receive a deportation order, commonly called a removal order, then ICE will put you on a plane or bus to your home country. It is possible that the judge may also allow you to "voluntarily" depart. If the judge allows you to voluntarily depart the United States, you usually have a certain number of days to pack your stuff and leave the country on your own and you will not have a deportation order or a removal order on your record.

If you are ordered deported, you may be able to appeal your case to higher courts—usually the Board of Immigration Appeals and the Federal Circuit Court of Appeals.

ABBREVIATED DEPORTATION PROCEEDINGS/EXPEDITED REMOVAL

Some people have even fewer rights than those available in the deportation or removal process. For example, those who are found at an airport without proper documents or within a hundred miles of the border without proper documents and cannot prove that they have been in the United States for more than fourteen days are placed in expedited removal. Under expedited removal, you can generally be deported without any hearing or opportunity to appeal.

How can I find out the date and location of my next immigration hearing?

Call the Immigration Court's toll-free number, (800) 898-7180, for information on your next hearing. You will need your A number (your individual immigration file number with the Department of Homeland Security, which contains seven or eight digits preceded by the letter *A*), which is listed on most immigration documents, to get recorded information about your case or your hearing.

What are my rights in a deportation proceeding?

ICE must tell you why you are in deportation proceedings and cannot keep you in jail for more than seventy-two hours without issuing a notice to appear against you, which is described earlier in this chapter (see page 74). If you remain silent and do not give them any information, ICE might not have any proof that you are here illegally, might not have any reason to deport you, and may be forced to release you.

In most cases, ICE cannot deport you without giving you the opportunity to have a hearing before an immigration judge. This hearing is very important for you if you have any possibility of remaining in the United States. If, however, you are undocumented (not here legally) and you are found within a hundred miles of the border and have been here for less than fourteen days, or you have certain criminal convictions or a prior deportation order, you do not have a right to a hearing before an immigration judge.

You have the right to a lawyer or accredited representative to represent you in deportation proceedings. However, the government will not pay for your lawyer. You must pay for a lawyer's services yourself. ICE should provide you with a list of local, free legal services that may be able to help you with your case. If you don't get it, ask for a copy.

You have a right to have a translator at your hearing. The immigration court will provide you with a translator during the hearing. The entire immigration hearing and all of the documents that the immigration court and ICE give you will be in English.

In most cases, you have the right to speak with a consular official from your home country, but not if you were deported through expedited removal.

If you are in immigration detention, you may have the right to a reasonable bond amount—the money you can pay to be released from jail while your case is pending. In many cases, ICE must set a reasonable bond amount so that you can go free while awaiting a hearing before an immigration judge. If you think your bond is set too high, you can ask for a hearing with an immigration judge to lower or eliminate the bond.

If you are about to be deported and you need help, remember that you should tell ICE that you want a lawyer (they should provide you with a list of local free legal services) and that you want to meet with the consular official from your home country.

CRIMINAL ARRESTS AND CONVICTIONS

Even if you're not deported, criminal acts that lead to an arrest or conviction can either permanently or temporarily prevent you from becoming a U.S. citizen or permanent resident, or from obtaining other legal immigration statuses. You can also be put into mandatory detention far away from your home and family until ICE deports you, or you can be prevented from reentering the United States after leaving for a trip outside the country, even if you're a longtime permanent resident.

JUVENILE CRIMES ARE NOT AS SERIOUS AS ADULT CRIMINAL CONVICTIONS

Criminal violations committed by juveniles generally do not have the same harsh immigration consequences as do convictions that adults receive in criminal court. Exceptions are juvenile crimes related to prostitution, severe sexual crimes, and certain drug crimes, especially if they involve drug sales. These criminal issues can be immigration problems—even for juveniles.

What places should I avoid if I have a prior criminal arrest or record?

If you have had any contact with the criminal justice system, including even just an arrest with no conviction, **you should NOT do any of the following until you speak to an experienced immigration lawyer or accredited representative:**

- Do not apply to become a U.S. citizen or permanent resident or apply to obtain any other immigration status.
- Do not go into an immigration office to ask questions or to renew your visa or green card.
- Do not leave the country or travel near the border or where there are border control checkpoints.
- Avoid contact with the criminal justice system or any immigration official.

Can I come back to the United States after being deported?

After being deported, you may be unable to return to the United States for the rest of your life. Only in some cases can you apply to return if you qualify for a waiver. Even then you must wait years outside of the United States before you can even apply, and there is no guarantee that you will receive permission to return or you will be able to apply for a waiver or pardon and be allowed back into the United States. It is very complicated and potentially risky to return to the United States if you have been deported in the past, so you should consult an experienced immigration lawyer or accredited representative for help.

If you reentered the United States illegally after having received an order of deportation or removal, you may simply be removed again without a hearing. Depending on why you were deported, you also may face time in federal prison for illegally

WARNING TO THOSE IN CRIMINAL COURT

If you have a criminal case pending against you and you are not a U.S. citizen, you should tell your public defender or criminal defense lawyer about your immigration status and that you need to know the immigration consequences of your case. Your request should alert your defense lawyer that there could be immigration consequences in your case and that they need to try to resolve your case in ways that won't make you deportable, ineligible for future immigration benefits, or identifiable to ICE for deportation proceedings. If you are in jail during your criminal court proceedings and an ICE officer comes to interview you, do not answer any questions, do not lie, and do not sign anything without speaking first to an experienced immigration lawyer or accredited representative. Do not say your name and do not say anything about where you were born or how you entered the United States. You simply can tell the ICE officer that you do not want to speak and that you want to talk to your lawyer.

reentering the country after being deported for certain crimes, face deportation again at the end of your sentence, and be disqualified from any immigration pardon.

EXAMPLE: *Miguel was deported in 1994. He came back to the United States in 1998 using fake papers. Earlier this year he got married and now he wants to apply for a green card through his U.S. citizen wife. Is it safe for him to do that? No! When he appears for his immigration interview (or any other time that he comes into contact with immigration authorities), they can just arrest him and use his old deportation order to remove him from the country.*

This area of the law is currently undergoing change. Hopefully there will be more immigration options available for people who have old orders of deportation or removal, but that is NOT now the case.

> **WARNING:** If you were ever deported, or ever picked up by an immigration officer at the border and taken back to your home country, you should talk to an experienced immigration lawyer or accredited representative before having any contact with immigration!

What is immigration detention?

Immigration detention is immigration jail in which noncitizens usually must stay until they are either deported or win their deportation case. Immigration detention can be at a local jail, private prison, or federal immigration detection center.

When can I be detained?

There are several situations that can lead to you, as a noncitizen, being detained and put into deportation proceedings. They include:

- You are stopped at the airport after having returned from traveling abroad;
- You are interviewed by immigration authorities while in jail either while waiting for your criminal case to end or serving a sentence in jail or prison;
- You are applying for an immigration benefit such as U.S. citizenship, legal permanent residence, or other visas;
- You have prior orders of deportation. The government currently is conducting operations to find and detain people with prior orders.

- Raids at home, at work, and on the street. ICE has certain priorities in conducting raids: they focus on immigrants who they know are already deportable, including those who use false Social Security numbers to obtain work, those with criminal records, those with prior deportation orders, and those with alleged gang affiliations. While tracking down these individuals, ICE targets others in the area who they think are undocumented and deportable. These arrests are called "collateral arrests."

How can I locate someone who is in immigration detention?

If you have the person's name and immigration identification number, or A number, you can call the local deportation office and ask them where the person is located. You can find the number for the local deportation office by calling the headquarters of the Office of Detention and Removal Operations at (202) 305-2734. Remember that people can be detained close to, or very far from, their homes at immigration detention sites, local jails, or other sites with which the government has contracted.

What might ICE do when they arrest and/or detain me?

An ICE officer generally will not tell you about your rights and usually will ask you questions about your legal status in this country. If ICE legally gets this information from you, they can use this information to deport you—and they often get the necessary information by just asking you. It is thus very important that you remain silent until you speak to a lawyer because there might be some possibilities for you to remain in the United States or you may have other rights that you might not know about.

You may be asked to sign an order of voluntary departure. Signing this piece of paper usually means that you will immediately have to leave the United States. ICE even might threaten to put you in jail for a long time if you do not sign this paper. ICE should not make these threats and you should continue to refuse to sign this paper until you speak to an experienced immigration lawyer or accredited representative.

You also may be asked to sign a paper admitting that you were using documents such as a fake green card, passport, birth certificate, certificate of U.S. citizenship, or Social Security card. Again, do not sign this paper without first speaking to an experienced immigration lawyer or accredited representative. Signing the paper may result in negative consequences and you may be deported from the United States without the possibility of ever returning.

What should I do if ICE arrests or detains me?

Don't say anything until you've spoken with an attorney or accredited representative.

YOU HAVE THE RIGHT TO REMAIN SILENT. Do not answer any questions. If you are undocumented, do not tell them your name or say anything about where you were born or how you entered the United States. You can simply tell them that you do not want to speak to them and would rather talk to a lawyer.

Insist on talking to an experienced immigration lawyer or accredited representative. If you do not have a lawyer or accredited representative, you can ask the ICE officer for a list of free or low-cost lawyers. Do not show ICE any documents, except a letter from a lawyer.

Do not sign anything, especially an order of voluntary departure or any admission that you were using fake documents, without first talking to an experienced immigration lawyer or accredited representative.

Tell the ICE official that you want a hearing in the city closest to where you live where there is an immigration court (so that they do not transfer your case and move you far away from friends and family).

You have the right to make a telephone call after you are arrested.

What should I do if ICE comes to my house?

DO NOT OPEN THE DOOR. Ask to see a search warrant, which is an order from a judge giving ICE permission to enter your home, or an arrest warrant, which is an order giving ICE permission to arrest someone named in the warrant. If the ICE official does not show you a search or arrest warrant, you do not have to open the door and you do not have to give them permission to enter your home.

If they produce a warrant, you must let them enter. Even if they have a search or arrest warrant and enter your home, you have the right to remain silent. Do not answer questions. Do not tell them your name or say anything about where you were born or how you came to the United States. You can simply tell them that you do not want to speak to them and would rather talk to a lawyer.

Again, do not sign anything, especially an order of voluntary departure, without first talking to an experienced immigration lawyer or accredited representative. Do not show any documents if the officials do not show you a search warrant.

What if I am undocumented and ICE raids my workplace?

YOU HAVE THE RIGHT TO REMAIN SILENT. Stay calm and do not run. You can quietly leave an area that ICE has entered. Do not answer questions or tell them anything about where you were born or how you came to the United States. You simply can tell them that you do not want to speak or that you want to talk to a lawyer. Do not sign anything, especially an order of voluntary departure, without first talking to an experienced immigration lawyer or accredited representative.

What if I am undocumented and an ICE officer stops me on the street?

DO NOT RUN AWAY. If an ICE officer or other immigration officer begins to ask you questions while you are walking down the street or in another public place such as a park, you can continue walking. ICE officers have to let you keep walking if they do not have a "good" reason to continue asking you questions. (One such "good" reason is if they have previously found many undocumented workers in the area.) They cannot stop you just because you are Latino or because you have an accent. Remember that you have the right to be silent. Whatever you do, do not run. If you run, you give them a good reason to stop you.

What if an ICE officer stops me in my car and wants to search it?

An ICE officer needs a good reason to stop you and search your car. A good reason to stop your car includes the fact that you violated a traffic law such as speeding. Once your car has been stopped, ICE must have a good reason to search your car without a search warrant. A good reason includes the fact that an ICE agent sees drugs in your car. If ICE has a good reason for stopping you, they can search your car without a search warrant. If they don't have a good reason and do not have a search warrant, it is very important not to give them permission to search your car.

If the police stop you, you do not have to show them any

papers except a driver's license and the car's registration. The police should not ask you any questions about your legal status in this country and should not demand to see immigration papers. If they ask you about your immigration status, assert your right to remain silent.

What are my rights at the border?

You have fewer and different rights at the border than you do in the interior of the United States. Remember that the "border" includes not only the line between the United States and Mexico or Canada, but also airports in all parts of the United States and areas close to the border. For example, there are border checkpoints throughout parts of Southern California. In these places, ICE can detain you to ask you more questions and you have to prove that you have legal permission to enter or be in the United States. They also can search you or your bags without a search warrant. Remember that you always have the right to remain silent and you can insist on talking to a lawyer if you are in the United States. If you are at an airport and have not yet entered the country, you do not have the right to see a lawyer.

If I am undocumented, is it safe for me to call the police in an emergency?

If you are in a life-threatening or emergency situation, you should call the police. Most police will not report you to any immigration authorities simply for being undocumented. Most state and local police are not required to enforce immigration laws.

However, there is some risk in contacting the police. First, the police can report you to ICE if they want to (although a few cities have sanctuary ordinances so that the police generally will not report undocumented people—you should check your city). Second, the police departments of some cities already cooperate with ICE to report undocumented people. Third, bills have been introduced recently that would *require* state and local police to enforce immigration laws and report undocumented people, and a few states have signed agreements with the government to enforce immigration laws. You thus should keep track of changes in immigration policy.

5

What You Must Know About Your Green Card Once You Have It

Will I need to renew my green card?

Green cards are issued with an expiration date of ten years after the card was issued. This does not mean that you have to reapply for permanent resident status. It just means that every ten years you must apply to replace your card.

How can I get a copy of my immigration file?

Sometimes people need copies of their immigration files because they have lost their papers and need proof of their status to replace a green card or naturalization certificate or otherwise verify their status in the United States.

If at some point you need it, you can request a copy of your Immigration and Naturalization Service (INS) or Citizenship and Immigration Services (CIS) immigration file by submitting a Freedom of Information Act/Privacy Act request on Form G-639 to CIS. This form can be downloaded from the CIS Web site at www.uscis.gov. You do not need to send any money with your request.

How long can I be outside the United States and still be considered a U.S. permanent resident?

Although there is really no set time period that a permanent resident can be abroad and still be considered a permanent resident, many attorneys tell permanent residents that it is best not to be abroad for more than six months at a time. Yet in reality, the rules are far more complicated than this. A permanent resident is not allowed to "abandon" his or her permanent residence and expect to keep his or her green card. Generally, if a permanent resident has moved to live in another country or stays abroad for a very long time, the Immigration Service could claim that the person has "abandoned" his or her residence and could place the person in deportation proceedings for the express purpose of trying to take away his or her green card and deporting him or her. The Immigration Service and courts will look at the permanent resident's reason or intent for leaving the United States and the ties that the person kept to the United States while abroad in determining if a permanent resident has abandoned his or her residence. Although the amount of time the permanent resident was gone is important, it is not the only factor in determining abandonment. It is common that a permanent resident was gone on a temporary visit abroad (for a vacation or to take care of an ill relative) for more than six months and would not be in danger of abandonment, and it is possible that a permanent resident is gone for less than six months but with the intent to live abroad instead of merely visit, and be found to have abandoned his or her residence.

Generally, if you want to keep your green card but also want to travel you should:

- Not move to actually live in another country;
- Go abroad only if you intend to visit and return to the United States after a relatively short period of time;
- Keep ties to the United States such as a bank account, your home, clothes, your job, if possible, and you should continue to file taxes in the United States;
- Request permission to come back to the United States if you will be gone for a long period of time. You can make this request by filing a reentry permit, Form I-131, with CIS before leaving the United States.

If you plan to be abroad for more than six months, talk to a lawyer or accredited representative before leaving.

I have a green card but want to study abroad for a year. What can I do so I won't lose my green card?

Before you leave to live abroad, you should apply to CIS for a reentry permit at least thirty days before your departure date. As of September 2006, the application process involves sending to the CIS Nebraska Service Center Form I-131, a copy of your green card, two photographs, and the filing fee. Check the CIS Web site for current filing fees and other requirements, as they can change. If CIS approves your request for a reentry permit, they will mail it to you and it will be good for two years. Make sure the CIS has your current and correct address.

WARNING: NOTIFY CIS IF YOU CHANGE YOUR ADDRESS

The law says that you must notify CIS within ten days if you change your address. You do this by filing Form AR-11 with CIS. The form can be downloaded from the CIS Web site at www.uscis.gov and includes an address for filing the form. If possible, send the AR-11 via certified mail return receipt requested and make a copy of the AR-11 as proof that you filed the form. It is especially important to notify CIS of your change of address if you have an application pending with them, so you can be sure that any notices that CIS sends will reach you.

6

Traveling to the
United States

Y OU MAY HAVE many reasons to travel into and out of the
United States, whatever your immigration status. But you
may not be able to come and go as you please. Here's what you
can expect from immigration officials as you attempt travel.

**What will happen when I arrive in the United States with
my immigration documents?**

You will go through "inspection," meaning that your documents
will be reviewed by an immigration officer from the Customs and
Border Protection (CBP) branch of the Department of Homeland Security. CBP is responsible for making sure that people
who enter the United States are legally permitted to do so. They
are authorized to review the documents of people arriving at the
airports and at land borders and also have the authority to arrest
undocumented people traveling overland to the United States.

I've passed my green card interview at the consulate, and I'm coming to the United States. What will happen?

Once your application is approved at your consular processing interview, the consular officer will give you some papers, including an immigrant visa, in a sealed envelope that you need to show at the U.S. border where you will apply for admission. At the border, a CBP agent will stamp your passport and you will become a permanent resident as of the day you enter the country. You will receive your green card in the mail within a few months. Make sure that the government has your correct address.

> **WARNING:** You must enter the United States within six months of your immigrant visa interview or your immigrant visa will expire and you will not be admitted as a permanent resident.

I'm a permanent resident returning to the United States from a trip abroad. What will I need to show at the border?

You will need to show a passport and your current green (legal permanent resident, or LPR) card, even if you are coming in from Canada or Mexico. You also need to show that you are admissible.

If I'm already a permanent resident of the United States, why do I need to show I'm admissible?

As a permanent resident, you could be barred from returning to the United States after a trip abroad and could lose your permanent residence if:

- You abandoned your LPR status.
- You have been absent from the United States for more than

180 days (six months) and you fall under one of the inadmissibility grounds listed in chapter 2.

- You committed an illegal act after you left the United States.
- You left the United States while the government had you in proceedings to deport you or remove you to your home country.
- You committed a crime in the United States, unless you were granted a waiver by the government.
- You are attempting to or you entered without inspection (meaning without appearing before a CBP officer).

If you're told you're inadmissible for one of these reasons, you have the right to a hearing before an immigration judge, and you can present evidence to show that you should be admitted. You should hire an experienced immigration lawyer or accredited representative to represent you at your hearing if this ever happens to you. You should not waive or give up your right to a hearing.

I'm coming to the United States with a nonimmigrant visa or under the visa waiver program. What will happen to me at the border?

A CBP officer will inspect your documents to make sure they are valid, and if satisfied, he or she will admit you to the United States. How much time you are permitted to stay depends on the type of visa you have; this is discussed in chapter 1.

What documents should I have when I arrive?

You should have a passport that is valid for at least six months and a visa stamped in your passport that is valid, or you should be eligible to come to the United States without a visa under the visa waiver program. You also may need an approval notice for your visa, depending on the type of nonimmigrant visa you have. An approval notice is an official piece of paper from the U.S. government showing that your visa was approved.

What if the CBP official is not satisfied with my documents?

Several things could happen. You could be given the chance to withdraw your application for admission and return home, or you could be subjected to expedited removal, which is discussed in chapter 4.

If you are a permanent resident, you have a right to a hearing before an immigration judge, and you have a right to hire an attorney to represent you. The government will not pay for an attorney to represent you.

What is secondary inspection?

If the first CBP officer has additional questions for you, he or she will bring you to a room that is separate from the regular inspection booth. This is called secondary inspection.

If you are sent to secondary inspection, you will be questioned about your eligibility to be admitted to the United States. This can be a very frightening process. You should try to stay calm and answer the officer's questions to the best of your ability. You should not let a CBP officer persuade you to sign any document or statement that you do not understand or do not agree with. This is very important! Unfortunately, you do not have the right to an attorney at a secondary inspection station. If you are a permanent resident, or the CBP has not determined whether you are admissible, you may be given an appointment to go to "deferred inspection" after being questioned at primary or secondary inspection.

What is deferred inspection?

Deferred inspection is an appointment with a CBP officer, which may take place at a CBP office in an airport or border station or at another location. A person with a deferred inspection appointment is not considered "admitted" to the United States. Rather, the decision to determine admissibility is put off until the appointment. A person with a deferred inspection appointment will have some time to gather documents to prove admissibility, and can hire a lawyer or accredited representative to assist in document gathering. A lawyer or accredited representative can also go with the person to the deferred inspection interview, but his or her role is more restricted than at a hearing. The CBP officer at deferred inspection does not have to listen to what the lawyer has to say, but may do so anyway.

What does it mean to withdraw my application for admission?

This means that you can give up your intention to enter the United States and return to your home country. This option is not guaranteed, but you can sometimes choose it if the CBP officer allows.

What should I know about border patrol?

The border patrol is the part of CBP that functions usually between the United States ports of entry and has authority to stop people from entering the country and from illegally being in border areas of it. The border patrol operates not only at land borders to the United States but also at airports and within a hundred miles of any land or coastal border of the country. Border patrol officers can pick up and detain you if you do not have papers. They also can remove you if you have been in the

United States for fourteen days or less and are found within a hundred miles of any land or sea border within the country. If you are removed in this way, you will have an expedited removal order.

If you don't have papers:
- You have the right not to answer questions about your immigration status.
- You have the right to request an attorney.
- You have the right to request a hearing.

If you do have papers:
- You may wish to identify yourself and show your immigration papers, but you do not have to.
- You have the right not to answer questions about your immigration status.
- You have the right to request an attorney.
- You have the right to request a hearing.

If you are stopped by border patrol:
- Do not answer any questions. Unless you are in the United States with legal papers, don't say anything about where you were born or how you entered the United States.
- Do not show any documents, except a letter from a lawyer or accredited representative. Above all, do not show any false documents!
- Do not sign any papers without first talking to an experienced immigration lawyer or accredited representative.
- Tell the officer that you want to have a hearing, and that you want it to be in the city closest to where you live that has an immigration court (so your case won't be transferred far away).

What is a border crossing card?

A border crossing card, or BCC, is a card, available to Mexican nationals, that permits the card holder to enter the United States for up to thirty days. People with BCCs may travel up to twenty-five miles inside the U.S. border in most places, and up to seventy-five miles from the border if admitted at certain places in the state of Arizona. Old BCC cards that do not contain computerized information are no longer valid. A person with a BCC is not given an admission stamp or other document when entering the United States. The U.S. government is in the process of changing the document requirements for entry, and it is not clear if the BCC will continue to be issued. However, people who have them can still use them until they are canceled.

Who must have a passport to enter the United States?

As of November 2006, everyone arriving by airplane must have a valid passport to enter the United States. This was not always the case for Mexicans and Canadians, but now they are no longer exempt from the passport requirement. People arriving by sea or land may still be exempt from the passport requirement, but that is also likely to change soon.

7

How and Why Should
I Become a U.S. Citizen?

There are four ways you can become a U.S. citizen.

1. If you were born in the United States, you are automatically a U.S. citizen.
2. In some cases, you may have automatically become a U.S. citizen even if you were born outside the United States, if one or both of your parents were U.S. citizens when you were born. The citizenship rules for people born outside of the United States are very complicated. If you were not born in this country and you had a parent who was a U.S. citizen, you should talk to an experienced immigration lawyer or accredited representative to determine if you automatically became a U.S. citizen.
3. If you had a green card and were under eighteen years old when one or both of your parents were or became U.S. citizens, you may have automatically become a U.S. citizen

even if you were born outside the United States. The specific rules for becoming a U.S. citizen in this way are very complicated and you should talk to an experienced immigration lawyer or accredited representative to determine if you automatically became a U.S. citizen.

4. If you have a green card, you can apply to become a U.S. citizen through naturalization.

Why should I become a U.S. citizen?

There are many reasons to become a U.S. citizen.

- You can vote in U.S. elections and help shape national and local policies that affect you and your family.
- You can have a U.S. passport, which can make travel to other countries and assistance from the U.S. government easier when you are in another country.
- You can apply to immigrate more family members than you would be able to do as a lawful permanent resident. Generally, the process is faster for the relatives of citizens.
- You cannot be deported and you cannot be stopped from entering the United States.
- You can live in another country for as long as you want without it affecting your citizenship. (In contrast, lawful permanent residents can lose their status if they abandon their U.S. residence by living in another country.)
- You can hold public office and certain government jobs.
- You can receive government benefits such as food stamps and Supplemental Security Income (SSI) (support for the aged, blind, and disabled) as a U.S. citizen for a longer period of time.

What should I consider before I apply to become a U.S. citizen?

There are several factors to take into account, including:

- The naturalization process to get U.S. citizenship can be difficult for some people. For example, the requirements that you speak some English and answer questions about U.S. government and history during an interview with Citizenship and Immigration Services (CIS) can be challenging. However, you can take citizenship classes at local schools to help you prepare. If you have a disability that prevents you from learning English or U.S. history and government, you may be excused from these requirements.

- People with past immigration violations or criminal histories should be especially careful when considering becoming a U.S. citizen. When you apply for citizenship, CIS could discover that you have immigration problems or crime-related issues and try to deport you.

- You may have to give up your citizenship in your home country. The embassy of your home country can tell you if they permit dual citizenship.

- You may have problems owning or later purchasing property in your home country, depending on your home country's laws. Contact your embassy to find out more about this.

How do I qualify for U.S. citizenship?

There are eight requirements for becoming a U.S. citizen through naturalization:

1. You must be a lawful permanent resident (have a green card) for five years, and your green card must be valid.

2. You must have been living in the United States for at least the last five years as a green card holder and been living for at least three months in the state or CIS district where you are applying.
3. You must have been physically present within the United States as a green card holder for at least half of the last five years (that is, thirty of the last sixty months).
4. You must show that you have "good moral character" for the five-year period before the date on which you apply for naturalization and during the entire naturalization process until you are sworn in as a U.S. citizen.
5. You must be at least eighteen years old.
6. You must pass a test showing that you are able to speak, read, and write ordinary English.
7. You must pass a test on U.S. history and government.
8. You must take an oath of allegiance to the United States and the principles of the U.S. Constitution.

Does a valid green card help naturalization?

Having a valid green card means you didn't commit fraud to get into the United States and you are not in deportation or removal proceedings. It also means that you haven't moved to another country while being a green card holder. If you have moved to another country, CIS could claim that you "abandoned your residence in the United States," and could place you in deportation proceedings. You can often avoid the determination that you abandoned your residence if you file a reentry permit, Form I-131, with CIS before leaving the United States.

Can I leave the country while awaiting naturalization?

You have to live in the United States continuously for at least the last five years as a green card holder before qualifying for naturalization. But you are allowed to take vacations outside the country and still qualify to naturalize. If you leave the country for between six and twelve months at a time during any one trip after getting your green card, CIS may ask you to prove that your home is still in the United States before you can become a citizen. If you cannot prove this to the satisfaction of CIS, you will have to wait five years from the date you returned from your trip before you can reapply for naturalization.

> **EXAMPLE:** *Mauro was gone from the United States for an eleven-month period. He left on July 13, 2004, and returned on June 13, 2005. Because of this absence, CIS denied his naturalization application and determined that he had broken the continuity of his residence. In this instance, Mauro must wait five years from the time he returned to the United States before he can reapply for naturalization. Thus, Mauro can apply for naturalization on June 13, 2010.*

Another rule states that if you left the country for more than a year at any time during the last five years, you have broken the continuity of your residence and cannot become a citizen. The rule states that you must wait four years and one day after having returned to the United States from your trip in order to apply for naturalization.

> **EXAMPLE:** *Mauro was gone from the United States for a thirteen-month period. He left on July 13, 2005, and returned on August 15, 2006. Because his absence broke the continuity of his residence, he must wait four years and one day from the time he returned to the United States before he can apply for naturalization. Thus, Mauro can apply for naturalization on August 16, 2010.*

If you made your home outside the United States at any time since you got your green card, CIS may decide you have abandoned or given up your lawful U.S. residence and may try to deport you. If at any time you moved from the United States to live in another country, you must speak with an experienced immigration lawyer or accredited representative before trying to apply for naturalization.

> **EXAMPLE:** *Hector lived in the United States with a green card for fifteen years. About eight years ago, he decided to move his family back to Mexico. He gave up his apartment, quit his job, took his children out of school, and they all moved to Mexico, where they have lived for two years. While in Mexico, Hector and his wife bought a small house, got jobs, and their children all went to school, and then they moved back to the United States. If Hector applies for naturalization he could be denied and placed in deportation proceedings and even deported for abandoning his green card status in the United States. Some attorneys may counsel that it may be best for Hector not to ever apply for naturalization. Thus, Hector must see an experienced immigration lawyer or accredited representative before applying for naturalization.*

When can I apply for naturalization?

If you've had your green card for five years, you can generally apply for naturalization three months before you will be eligible to naturalize.

> **EXAMPLE:** *Tomas has had his green card since January 10, 2006. Tomas will be eligible for naturalization on January 10, 2011. Yet Tomas can apply for naturalization three months early. Thus, Tomas can apply for naturalization on October 10, 2010.*

How do I calculate if I have enough time in the United States to naturalize?

No matter how long you have been living in the United States, you must still be able to show that you actually have been here for at least half of the last five years; that is, thirty out of the last sixty months. Thus, during the last five years, the number of days you spent outside the United States cannot be more than the number of days you spent inside the United States.

> **EXAMPLE:** *Mary was denied naturalization because during the last five years (sixty months) she had been physically present in the United States for only twenty-four months. Mary must wait and reapply when she has been physically present in the United States for at least thirty of the sixty months prior to the time she reapplies.*

THE "GOOD MORAL CHARACTER" REQUIREMENT

You must be able to show "good moral character" for the five years before applying for naturalization and during the naturalization process. If you have committed certain types of crimes, told a U.S. official that you were a U.S. citizen when you were not, helped other people enter the country illegally, voted or registered to vote in an election in the United States and were ineligible to vote, have ever been ordered deported (to leave the United States) by a judge, did not pay all taxes required of you, did not provide financial support for your children, as required, and received government assistance (such as food stamps) when you were ineligible to do so, you could have problems with your naturalization case.

> **EXAMPLE:** *Elena applied for naturalization on September 13, 2008. To qualify she must show she has had good moral character*

during the entire five-year period before applying and during the entire naturalization process. Thus, she must show she has good moral character from September 13, 2003, until September 13, 2008, and also during the entire naturalization application process.

What should I check before I apply for naturalization?

When you apply for naturalization, you invite CIS to review your whole criminal history (which they will get from the FBI), your whole immigration history (which they will get from their files), and other facts about you. As the government reviews your application, CIS may realize that you have immigration or criminal problems that can keep you from becoming a U.S. citizen. They might even find a legal reason to take away your green card and deport you.

Before you apply to naturalize and try to become a citizen of the United States, be sure that there is nothing about you that can cause you problems with CIS. If you think you may have a problem, it does not mean you can't apply for naturalization. But you should speak with an experienced immigration lawyer or accredited representative first. If you answer yes to any of the following questions, you must talk to an experienced immigration lawyer or accredited representative before applying for naturalization:

- Have you ever been arrested (by the police, Immigration and Naturalization Service [INS], Bureau of Immigration and Customs Enforcement [ICE], Customs and Border Protection [CBP], or the Department of Homeland Security), convicted of a crime, or had to deal with the police *in any way*?
- Have you left the United States for more than six months since getting your green card?

- Have you ever moved your home to another country since getting your green card?
- If you obtained your green card through your parent, were you married at the time, but claimed you were not?
- Did you give false information, or withhold information, on your application for permanent residence?
- Have you ever helped or encouraged anyone to cross the border illegally (without papers)?
- Have you entered the United States without passing through inspection since getting your green card?
- Have you ever given false information or withheld infomation to get (or continue to get) welfare or other public benefits?
- Have you failed to register for the military draft in the United States if you were required to? (All men, except those on non-immigration visas such as a student or visitor visa, including non-U.S. citizens and even those without legal immigration papers, are required to do so between the ages of eighteen and twenty-six.)
- Have you ever failed to financially support your dependent children or husband or wife?
- Have you ever said you were a U.S. citizen?
- Have you ever voted or registered to vote in the United States?
- Have you ever failed to pay your taxes?
- Have you ever been a member of the Communist Party in or outside of the United States?
- Have you ever been deported or been in deportation proceedings?

If I become a U.S. citizen through naturalization, can my under-age-eighteen child become a U.S. citizen, too?

Yes, in some cases, if you became a U.S. citizen through the naturalization process and your child is under eighteen and has a green card, he or she may have automatically become a U.S. citizen through the citizenship of one of his or her parents. The specific rules for becoming a U.S. citizen in this way are very complicated, and you and your child must see an expert in immigration law to determine if he or she automatically became a U.S. citizen through your citizenship.

How will I have to show I can speak, read, and write ordinary English?

Although you will not be required to speak, read, or write *perfect* English, you will have to answer interview questions in English about what you wrote on your application form and about U.S. history and government. You will also have to write a simple sentence in English. At your interview, you may be required to read out loud parts of your application, some simple sentences, or something from the set of U.S. history and government test questions. Check www.uscis.gov for information about the written English test.

Are there any exceptions to the English–speaking rule?

There are three exceptions:

- At the time of applying for naturalization, if you are fifty-five years old or older and have been living in the United States with a green card for at least fifteen years, then you do not have to speak, read, or write any English to become a U.S. citizen.
- At the time of applying for naturalization, if you are fifty years old or older and have been living in the United States with a green card for at least twenty years, then you do not have to speak, read, or write any English to become a U.S. citizen.

- If you have a physical or mental disability that prevents you from speaking, reading, or writing English, you may ask CIS to excuse you from these requirements. CIS calls this a waiver of the English requirements. To be granted this waiver, you need to submit Form N-648, which must be completed by a medical doctor or doctor of osteopathy or a clinical psychologist. It is advised that you consult with an experienced immigration lawyer, accredited representative, or trusted community-based organization before completing this form.

EXAMPLE: *Lupe is fifty-six years old and has been a green card holder for seventeen years. She doesn't need to learn English to become a U.S. citizen because on the day she submitted her naturalization application, she was over fifty-five years old and had been a green card holder for over fifteen years.*

WARNING: Learning English is important and is very helpful to you because it makes it easier for you to pass the citizenship test, makes it harder for some people to take advantage of you, may help you get a job, facilitates your participation in community affairs, and makes it easier for you to know what is going on. To find out about English classes, call your local community-based organization, local school district office, or local high school or adult school.

What is the test on U.S. history and government?

In order to become a naturalized U.S. citizen, you must pass a test on U.S. history and government. Essentially, this means you must answer some questions during your naturalization interview about U.S. history and government. The questions will be taken from a list of a history and government questions that is available at community agencies helping with naturalization cases and at the CIS Web site (www.uscis.gov).

Are there any exceptions to the test requirement?

If you have a physical or mental disability that prevents you from demonstrating that you know U.S. history and government, you may ask CIS to excuse you from these requirements. This process is called a waiver. You need to submit Form N-648, which must be completed by a medical doctor or doctor of osteopathy or a clinical psychologist. It is advised that you consult with an experienced immigration lawyer, accredited representative, or trusted community-based organization before completing this form.

> **EXAMPLE:** *Ana was in a car accident and suffered significant head injuries. Because of these injuries, she cannot talk or hear, and forgets things easily. Ana can still naturalize. She will not have to learn English or U.S. government and history so long as she gets a doctor to complete the disability waiver form proving her medical disability.*

Some people are able to take an easier U.S. history and government test. If you are sixty-five years old or older and have been a lawful permanent resident for at least twenty years, you will be asked questions from a list of twenty-five possible questions that are easier than the full list of questions. You will be allowed to answer these questions in your mother language. Go to www.uscis .gov to get a list of these questions. They are available in English, Spanish, and Chinese.

What is the oath of allegiance to the United States and attachment to the principles of the U.S. Constitution?

During your naturalization interview and as part of your naturalization application, you will have to answer several questions about your attachment to the United States, especially your support of the U.S. Constitution and willingness to defend the United States. After CIS approves your application, you will have to take an oath of allegiance showing your support for the United States.

What if my religion forbids me to take an oath of allegiance to the United States? Can I still become a naturalized citizen?

Yes, if your religion does not allow you to take certain oaths, you can ask CIS to modify the oath to fit your religious constraints. Please be aware that only a few religions truly forbid people from taking such an oath.

What if I have a medical disability such that I cannot understand the oath of allegiance?

There is an exception to the rule of having to take the oath of allegiance if you have a mental or physical problem that keeps you from understanding the oath of allegiance. It is advisable that you get a letter from your doctor indicating that you will be unable to take the oath due to a disability.

Are there different requirements for naturalization if I am married to a U.S. citizen?

Yes, the requirements for becoming a U.S. citizen through naturalization are a bit easier if you are married to a U.S. citizen. But these easier requirements only apply if before you submit your naturalization application you have been living with and married to your U.S. citizen spouse for at least three years and your spouse has been a U.S. citizen for at least three years.

The easier requirements for spouses of U.S. citizens include:

- You have had your green card for only three years instead of five before qualifying for naturalization. You can apply three months before you qualify for naturalization.
- You have been physically present in the United States for only eighteen months (one and a half years) instead of thirty months (two and a half years).
- You have had good moral character for thirty-six months instead of sixty months.

The other requirements are the same whether you are married to a U.S. citizen or not. Thus, you still have to have lived in the CIS area (called a district) or state in which you are applying for three months before applying; take the English and U.S. history and government tests unless you fall into the exceptions stated above; and take the loyalty oath to the United States.

> **EXAMPLE:** *José obtained his status as a green card holder in 2006. In 2007, he married someone who had been a U.S. citizen all of her life. Assuming they remain married and living together for three years, José will become eligible for naturalization in 2010, three years after his marriage. If he were to get divorced before he applied for naturalization, he would have to wait until 2011, the full five years, before qualifying for naturalization.*

Does being in the military help me become a U.S. citizen?

Yes, being in the military can help you become a U.S. citizen. For instance, instead of having to wait five years as a green card holder to become eligible for naturalization, if you are still on active duty in the U.S. military or have served honorably in the U.S. military within the last six months, you will need to wait for only one year as a green card holder in order to be eligible for naturalization. There are other easier requirements for people serving in the military. Please see the CIS Web site (www.uscis.gov), ask a reputable agency in your town, or talk with the immigration point of contact at your military base.

Additionally, if you served in the military during certain periods of war, for example, during the war in Iraq, you could become a U.S. citizen even though you were never a green card holder. Check the CIS Web site (www.uscis.gov) for more information on this subject.

There is no fee if you file your naturalization application under the military naturalization program.

Are the rules for becoming a U.S. citizen different if I obtained my green card through the asylum or refugee process?

Yes, one main rule differs if you obtained your green card through the asylum or refugee process. Instead of having to be a green card holder for five years before qualifying for naturalization, if you obtained your green card through asylum you only have to wait four years after becoming a permanent resident to be eligible for naturalization. If you obtained your green card as a refugee, you have to wait only four years from the date you entered the United States as a refugee.

How do I apply for naturalization?

There are three basic steps to becoming a naturalized citizen:

1. Determine whether you are eligible to become a U.S. citizen. Do you meet the requirements? Do you have any is-

sues that will cause problems with CIS? If you think you may have a problem, you might still be able to apply but *first* talk to an experienced immigration lawyer or accredited representative.

2. Complete the naturalization application form (Form N-400). See www.uscis.gov for information on obtaining immigration forms.

3. Mail in your application. Send your application and documents to the correct CIS office. The instructions on the naturalization application explain exactly how to complete the form and how to find out where to send it.

What should I include with my naturalization application?

- Your completed naturalization form (the N-400 form). Make sure all spaces are filled out and you have signed it.

- A check or money order payable to the Department of Homeland Security. Write your alien registration number ("A number") and "N-400" in the memo section of the check. The fee changes constantly. You can find the required fee at the CIS office in your area or on the CIS Web site at www.uscis.gov.

- Two passport photographs of yourself. Write your name and "A" number on the back of each photo in pencil. Put them in a sealed envelope or in a small plastic bag (so they won't get separated) and attach them to your application packet.

- A copy of your lawful permanent resident card (green card). Include a copy of both sides of the card.

- Send your application as certified mail, return receipt requested. This can be done at any post office for a few dollars and can help you prove that CIS received it.

- *Always keep photocopies of everything that you send to CIS.*

What if I can't afford the fee?

If you are low-income and don't have enough money to pay the application fee, you can request that CIS waive the fee. For information on how to apply for a fee waiver, talk to a community agency in your area or go to the CIS Web site at www.uscis.gov.

What happens after I file my application?

After you file your application, you will get a notice from CIS telling you where and when to get your fingerprints taken. When you go to have your fingerprints taken, bring with you your green card and another form of identification (like a driver's license) with your picture on it.

In most parts of the country, you will have to wait about six to twelve months for your naturalization interview. CIS will mail you just one notice of when and where your interview will take place, normally about a month before the interview.

Make sure to prepare for your interview by studying English, U.S. government and history, and the answers you wrote on your naturalization application. Usually, you will be able to find English classes and citizenship preparation classes at a school in your community.

If you move, call the CIS at (800) 870-3676 to change your address, or change it on the Web site (www.uscis.gov); do a search for "Address Change" and follow the instructions. You will also need to get a change-of-address form (AR-11). Changing your address is very important because you do not want to miss your

WARNING: Do not present yourself to the CIS if you don't have legal immigration papers!

notice for an interview. If possible, ask someone at your old address to keep watch for any mail from CIS.

What if I don't hear from CIS for a long time after I filed my application?

This is a good reason to seek an InfoPass appointment with the CIS, as discussed in chapter 1. Other reasons for seeking an appointment include if there is a change in your address or if you are confused about the status of your application. If you have moved, be sure to file a change-of-address form with the appropriate offices. Not having filed a change-of-address form could explain why you haven't heard anything.

What if I'm scheduled for an interview but I can't go on that date?

While you can have your interview rescheduled, this request could create a very long delay. It thus usually is best to go to the interview when scheduled. If you can't make it, send a letter to the CIS office where your interview is scheduled before the appointment date by certified mail, return receipt requested, asking for a new date and time. Include in the letter the reason why you need a new interview date.

What if I missed my scheduled interview without writing to CIS in advance?

You may still be able to get another interview scheduled if it is within one year of your original interview date. If it is within thirty days of your original interview, your chances are even better. Write a letter to CIS telling them why you missed the interview and asking for a new interview date.

What should I expect during my interview?

The CIS officer will ask you questions about the information on the application and five to ten questions from the CIS list of questions about U.S. history and government. The officer will test your English by asking you to answer questions during the interview, write a few dictated sentences, and read something out loud.

If the officer finds any problems with your application, he or she may ask you either to fill out forms at the interview or to complete them at home and send them back to CIS. He or she may ask you to bring other documents as well. If you have to bring back documents to CIS, you will get a special form called an N-14, which will indicate what CIS needs and when you must send it back.

What should I take with me to the interview?

The government will send you a list of the documents you need to bring. Be sure to take your green card, passport (if you have one), an identification card (like a driver's license) that includes your picture, tax records, your marriage or divorce certificate, if you have them, and an original of any court disposition. You also should take a copy of your naturalization application so you can study it before your interview.

What will happen if my application is approved?

If CIS approves your application, you should receive a notice indicating that you have been approved and giving you an appointment for a "swearing in" ceremony. CIS may give you the notice during your interview or they may mail it to you. Answer the questions on the back of the notice and bring it with you to the swearing-in ceremony along with your green card, which you need to return to CIS because they will not let you keep it once you are a citizen. At the ceremony, you and all of the other naturalization applicants must promise loyalty (pledge allegiance) to the United States. You will get your certificate of naturalization the same day.

Once I go to the swearing-in ceremony and take the oath of allegiance, can I register to vote and apply for a U.S. passport?

Yes. You can register to vote at the Department of Motor Vehicles (DMV), your county registrar of voters' office, and other locations. In fact, there might be opportunities to register at the swearing-in ceremony. It is very important that you register to vote so you can help choose your elected officials, such as the president of the United States, your state's governor, and your local community representatives.

Also, once you get your naturalization certificate, you can get a U.S. passport. Sometimes, the passport agency helps people complete the paperwork immediately following the swearing-in ceremony. You also can apply for a passport at many U.S. post offices.

Why would CIS deny my application?

There are many reasons why CIS might deny your application, including:

- *You did not pass the English or U.S. history and government test.* This is one of the most common reasons people do not get approved. If this happens, CIS will automatically give you another interview two to three months after your first interview, during which you will have another opportunity to answer the questions.

- *CIS needs more information.* A CIS officer sometimes will ask you for documents to prove something in your application, such as an arrest record or a letter from a government agency. The officer will give you a form, called an N-14, that says which documents are needed and when they are due at CIS. If you submit them within the time limit, and they do not show that you have problems with your application, CIS will send you a notice telling you that you have been approved, and CIS will schedule you for a swearing-in ceremony. If you do not send the documents in on time, or if they show that you have a problem with your application, your application might be denied.

- *CIS believes there is a problem with your good moral character.* CIS may deny your application for naturalization if they decide that you do not have good moral character for some of the reasons listed earlier in this chapter (see page 105).

- *You haven't lived for a sufficient amount of time in the United States with a green card.* CIS may deny your application if they determine you have not been living in the United States for five years with a green card, or, if you married a U.S. citizen, three years.

What can I do if my naturalization application is rejected?

You can appeal the denial if you think you were wrongly denied. The appeal is called a Request for Hearing on a Decision in Naturalization Proceedings. You have thirty days to appeal the case. Or, you can start the application process again and reapply for naturalization. Of course, if you reapply you would have to pay the application fee again.

EXAMPLE: *Marta applied for naturalization but was denied because she had her green card for four years and eight months be-*

fore applying for naturalization, instead of the required four years and nine months. She has thirty days to decide to appeal her case or not and then submit her appeal. After consulting with a lawyer, Marta decided it was best not to appeal because she had applied too early and thus wasn't eligible then for naturalization. Rather than waste her money on an appeal that would just be denied anyway, she decided to reapply for naturalization. She is now eligible to apply for naturalization because she has had her green card for more than four years and nine months.

8

Getting Help with Immigration Concerns

Your friends, family members, and coworkers may have experience with immigration issues. But it would be a mistake to take their advice—no matter how well-meaning—because they may not have accurate or current information.

Immigration laws change often, and you should only count on experienced attorneys and accredited representatives to be up-to-date and best able to assist you.

Legally, only a lawyer or an accredited representative can give you legal advice on how to obtain a green card or other immigration-related concerns. Other people can help you fill out forms, but they are not legally allowed to give you advice.

What does it mean to be a lawyer?

Lawyers are licensed by a state bar association in the state in which they work. Sometimes a lawyer who is licensed in one state will practice immigration law in another state. This is allowed in

> **WARNING: WATCH OUT FOR IMMIGRATION SCAMS**
>
> Be careful when getting someone to help you with your immigration papers. Don't be fooled by false promises. You could lose your money *and* be removed or deported from the United States. Be careful of people who say they are *"notarios."* They are neither lawyers nor accredited representatives.

some states, but not in others. Most states require lawyers to tell you where they are licensed on their letterhead and business cards. You can check to see whether the lawyer you are consulting is licensed by checking with the state bar association in your state or the other state where the lawyer says he or she is licensed. If the lawyer is not licensed anywhere that you can find, or if he or she has been disciplined by the state bar for some kind of misconduct, you need to find someone else to represent you. Please understand that in the United States a *notario* is NOT a lawyer and is not allowed to give legal advice. A *notario* in the United States is someone who is allowed merely to notarize documents. A *notario* does not need any education, experience, or knowledge to perform his job, while a lawyer has to have attended four years of college and three years of law school, and then must pass a two- to three-day exam that is very difficult.

To check an attorney's credentials and to make sure he or she is in good standing with your state, visit the American Bar Association's Web site at www.abanet.org. I also recommend you contact the American Immigration Lawyers Association's Lawyer Referral Service at (800) 954-0254.

What does it mean to be an "accredited representative"?

This was discussed earlier in the book, but it's worth another mention. An accredited representative works for a nonprofit organization serving immigrants and has been authorized by the government to represent people with their immigration papers. This means that an accredited representative can give you legal advice, can help you prepare your immigration applications, and can appear with you at any interviews or hearings required before immigration officials or immigration judges. In other words, an accredited representative can do almost as much as an attorney can to assist you in immigration proceedings and applications. An accredited representative must tell you that this is what he or she is and show you proof if you ask for it.

CHOOSING SOMEONE TO HELP YOU

You need to be very careful when choosing someone to help you. Many people have been fooled into trusting the wrong person, and not only have lost money, but have ended up getting deported. It's best to go to an experienced immigration lawyer or to an accredited representative, but even then you should be careful. Even some lawyers have been known to be dishonest and have cheated their clients.

To find a lawyer to help you, call the local state bar association (you can find the number for your state bar in the phone book) or call the American Immigration Lawyers' Association at (800) 954-0254 for a referral to a lawyer in your area. If you have access to a computer, you can also look for the state bar of any state at www.google.com.

To find an accredited representative to help you, look for an International Institute, Catholic Charities, or other nonprofit legal services organization near you. These are three reputable national organizations that help immigrants with their papers. If they can't help you, they can usually tell you about an honest lawyer or other organization near you that may be able to help. You also can seek advice from respected people in your community, such as religious and community leaders, who may be able to suggest where you can find help.

FRAUD ALERT: IMMIGRATION SCAMS TO WATCH OUT FOR

Be careful if someone claims the following:

- You can apply for a green card because you have been here ten years.*
- There's a new amnesty, and anyone can apply.
- Your employer can apply for a green card for you, even if you have no legal immigration status.
- Your employer can apply for a green card for you, no matter what your job or skills are.
- I have contacts with businesses that can obtain a green card for you.
- You can apply for asylum to get a green card.

Most likely these are immigration scams. Protect yourself and don't be fooled. Get a second opinion from an experienced immigration lawyer or accredited representative.

---

*There is something called cancellation of removal, explained in chapter 1, that requires you to have ten years in the United States, good moral character, and a U.S. citizen parent, spouse, or child who will suffer "exceptional and extremely unusual hardship" if you are deported. It is very difficult to qualify for cancellation of removal, and you can apply for it only if you are already in removal proceedings before an immigration judge. Just having ten years here is NOT enough! Just being a good person is also NOT enough.

HOW TO AVOID A FRAUDULENT IMMIGRATION PROVIDER

Do not trust anyone who says any of the following:

- "We can get you work permits right away."
- "We offer 'no risk' immigration."
- "We can get U.S. visas for you and your family in a few weeks."
- "We know people at immigration and can get your papers done quickly."

U.S. immigration law is complicated and there are never any guarantees. An experienced immigration lawyer or accredited representative should be able to explain to you how and why you are eligible for any immigration benefit, and what risk you may face, if any.

Here is a list of important things to keep in mind when hiring someone to help you with your immigration papers:

- *Never* sign any blank application papers.
- *Never* sign any paper or immigration form that you do not fully understand. (Have someone you trust translate it for you.)
- *Always* demand a written contract for any immigration services when you are not working with an agency recognized by the government to provide immigration services.
- *Always* demand to have the amount the service is going to cost you specified in the contract.
- *Do not* sign a contract that you don't understand.
- *Watch out* for anyone who wants you to pay all of the fee immediately.
- *Always* get copies of the papers prepared for you.
- *Never* let anyone keep your original documents (example: birth certificates, marriage certificates).

- *Get* a receipt for any money you pay. (Make sure it has the amount paid, the date paid, your name, and the name of the person or business that you paid.)
- *Never* work with someone who will not answer your questions.

What if the fraud has already been committed?

If the person cheating you is a lawyer, call the state bar where the lawyer is licensed. In California, that number is (800) 843-9053. Every state has a state bar, which can be found in the telephone directory or online.

If the person cheating you is not a lawyer, you can call the district attorney's office in your county to complain. In California and Texas, the state attorney general's office may be able to help you. The phone number for the California Attorney General's Office of Immigration Assistance is (888) 587-0557. The phone number for the Texas Attorney General's Office is (800) 252-8011. Other state attorney generals' offices may or may not be able to help. You must look up the state attorney general's office in your state to find out. Each state has its own attorney general's office. This is NOT the same as the U.S. attorney general, who is the chief attorney for the entire United States.

9

Getting Involved

THERE ARE MANY ISSUES that affect you, your family, and your community, and you can take steps to work for each cause in which you believe. If you're a legal permanent resident or citizen, terrific. But even if you aren't, there are still things you can do to try to help make things better.

In the United States, many people try to impact the views of elected officials, including members of Congress, and influence what is in the media—that is, in the newspapers, on the radio and TV, and on the Internet.

It is important to participate in the debate on issues that have an effect on your life and those of your friends, family, and community. Why? Because the U.S. Congress passes laws that affect your life every day, and the media's portrayal of immigration and immigrants and their concerns helps mold how people think of you and your community. If you don't participate, others will. And your absence will give them the opportunity to portray you in ways that may not reflect who you are, and pass laws that will hinder rather than help you. Your presence in these debates will help ensure that your views are known, if not reflected, in policies and laws.

HOW TO GET INVOLVED

There are many ways you can effectively let people know what you believe and how you think local, state, and federal laws and policies should be changed to address your needs. People who work for social and political change are called advocates. An advocate works in support of something, to change laws and policies with government officials on all levels. Advocates also work in their communities to generate support for an issue or cause. Advocates understand that the media can be a tool to help them get out their points of view in their community and to the general public and elected officials.

Smart and successful advocacy involves working in the community, with elected officials, and with the media. It's based on the following ten steps.

1. **Set expectations accurately and strategically.**

   It is important to stay attuned to the environment, be flexible, and recognize the importance of short-, medium-, and long-term strategies and tactics that reflect these strategies.

   It also is important that you don't set your expectations too high or low. If you set them too high, you'll have a very hard time reaching your goals. You'll face a lot of disappointment and that will make it harder to motivate yourself and your colleagues. If you set your expectations too low, you will not be fulfilling your potential. Setting your expectations just right—because you accurately gauge the political environment, your targeted audiences, and your strengths and weaknesses—is essential to keeping yourself motivated, involved, and successful.

2. **Support the need for advocacy in the short and long term, and at the local, state, and national levels.**

   Pro-immigration advocates need to expend resources and energy to protect and expand the pro-immigration agenda in the short and long term because immigration is and will remain a top issue on the public agenda. Anti-immigration supporters know this, and they also understand the importance of focusing their efforts on the local as well as on the national level. Pro-immigration supporters need to do the same, working with elected officials, the media, and old and new allies.

3. **Be prepared to respond both proactively and reactively.**

   While it is important to never let a negative story go unanswered, it is also crucial that you initiate positive contacts with your elected officials and the media. In that way, you will set the stage on your own terms consistent with your own longer-term strategy.

4. **Know how to talk about our issues.**

   Immigration opponents use harsh rhetoric to scare people and generate fear. They equate immigrants with terrorists and talk about cities being flooded with immigrants, immigrants displacing Americans at work, ethnic tensions increased, and staggering costs faced especially by state and local governments.

   Pro-immigration advocates need to emphasize that immigrants are not terrorists, are central to the U.S. economy, and reflect the best of America's heritage and tradition. Immigration should be talked about in terms of family, opportunity, investment, and community and emphasize that immigration has made this country the best and brightest.

5. **Recognize the importance of training.**

   Central to advancing pro-immigration and immigrant agendas is mastering new skills that are not difficult to learn and can be helpful in other areas. Such skills involve effectively using new technologies, effectively knowing how to talk about your issues with different audiences, understanding the political process, and keeping up-to-date on what is going on in areas that impact your issues.

6. **Develop long-term relationships with elected officials and the media.**

   Developing these ongoing relationships is vital. Frequently contact your elected officials, educate them about immigration, inform them of the local impact of specific legislation, and invite them to address a community meeting, put them on your mailing list, and keep them informed about issues of concern to you and your community. And don't forget to thank them when they do a good job.

   A higher media profile will require pushing positive immigration-related stories and sympathetic cases, going on local radio shows, and writing op-eds and articles for local newspapers. Local TV networks welcome visual stores. Develop a relationship with your local newspaper and radio reporters. Pay attention to the newspapers, and find out who covers immigration issues. Invite them to an event, and make yourself available for interviews.

7. **Work in coalition with partners on specific issues.**
   Work in coalition at the local level on specific issues. Understand that other organizations may not share your entire agenda, and in fact may work to oppose you on some important issues, but can be powerful allies on other issues. Pro-immigration advocates need to work together with groups with whom they have shared causes, as well as with others who offer new opportunities and alliances, such as local businesses, education groups, and chambers of commerce.

8. **Take advantage of new technology.**
   Technology offers immigration advocates many opportunities, including the ability to communicate more easily and cheaply, work together more efficiently, and reach interested people, elected officials, and the general public more broadly. Opponents use technology to organize in the present and anticipate the future, so you need to do the same, and more.

9. **Encourage people to naturalize and register to vote.**
   It is vital that people naturalize, register to vote, and vote on Election Day. Encourage your friends, family members, and neighbors to participate by registering to vote and then showing up on Election Day.

10. **Feel empowered because you are!**

HOW A BILL CAN BECOME A LAW

The chart on the following page lays out one way a bill can become a law in the United States. A bill cannot become a law until the same measure is passed by both the U.S. House and Senate and is signed by the president. To find out more, please talk to a local community group or your religious leader. Please also remember that states and local governments pass laws and policies that impact you. It is important that you also understand how these entities make laws and policies.

How a Bill Can Become a Law

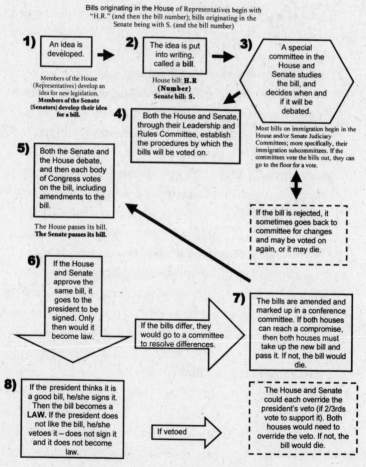

Bills originating in the House of Representatives begin with "H.R." (and then the bill number); bills originating in the Senate being with S. (and the bill number)

1) An idea is developed.

Members of the House (Representatives) develop an idea for new legislation. **Members of the Senate (Senators) develop their idea for a bill.**

2) The idea is put into writing, called a **bill**.

House bill: **H.R (Number)**
Senate bill: **S.**

3) A special committee in the House and Senate studies the bill, and decides when and if it will be debated.

Most bills on immigration begin in the House and/or Senate Judiciary Committees; more specifically, their immigration subcommittees. If the committees vote the bills out, they can go to the floor for a vote.

4) Both the House and Senate, through their Leadership and Rules Committee, establish the procedures by which the bills will be voted on.

5) Both the Senate and the House debate, and then each body of Congress votes on the bill, including amendments to the bill.

The House passes its bill. **The Senate passes its bill.**

If the bill is rejected, it sometimes goes back to committee for changes and may be voted on again, or it may die.

6) If the House and Senate approve the same bill, it goes to the president to be signed. Only then would it become law.

If the bills differ, they would go to a committee to resolve differences.

7) The bills are amended and marked up in a conference committee. If both houses can reach a compromise, then both houses must take up the new bill and pass it. If not, the bill would die.

8) If the president thinks it is a good bill, he/she signs it. Then the bill becomes a **LAW.** If the president does not like the bill, he/she vetoes it — does not sign it and it does not become law.

If vetoed

The House and Senate could each override the president's veto (if 2/3rds vote to support it). Both houses would need to override the veto. If not, the bill would die.

Developed by the Immigrant Legal Resource Center (ILRC). Updated 12/2006.

MEETING WITH AN ELECTED OFFICIAL

Face-to-face meetings with elected and appointed officials or other leaders are often the most effective way to influence them. You may want to meet them to educate them on the issues, ask them to become spokespeople for your point of view, ask them to cosponsor and/or support or oppose legislation, or urge them to moderate their opposition to a bill you support. Central to these activities is the primary goal of your seeking these meetings: to develop a relationship with your elected officials. If you are unable to meet in person with them, meet with their staff. They work on legislation, regulatory issues, and policy every day and greatly influence their bosses' positions and votes. Here are the components:

ARRANGING THE APPOINTMENT

- Call the official's office and ask to speak to the scheduler. Once connected to the scheduler, request an appointment. Note who you are and whom you represent, the purpose of the meeting, when you would like the meeting to take place (be flexible), and who will be attending. If you are speaking to the scheduler, and not the staffer who covers immigration, ask for the name and contact information of the immigration staffer.
- Some offices may ask you to send your request for a meeting in writing. If that is the case, get the name of the person who requested that you send the letter, send the letter promptly, and follow up with a phone call.
- If you're told the person you want to meet with is unavailable and will continue to be unavailable, don't give up. Reiterate your request to meet with a representative from that office who has knowledge of the issue for which you are calling. The scheduler might then suggest you talk with the staffer who

covers the issue of concern, be it immigration, health access, education, or whatever issue about which you are seeking the meeting. Ask to be connected with that person. You may end up meeting with someone who works for the person with whom you were seeking the meeting. Such a meeting is also important to have.

PREPARING FOR THE MEETING

- Do your homework. Know exactly what you want to say and carefully review your message. Research the elected officials with whom you are meeting so you know their positions on relevant issues.

- If you want other people to attend this meeting with you, select those who will contribute to the meeting because, for example, of who they are or know or because they have expertise in a relevant area. For example, a priest from the community, a local immigrant business leader, or an immigrant student would add an important voice to your meeting if you are focusing on an issue related to immigration.

- Prepare a packet of materials to give out that supports your position. These materials could include background information, fact sheets, and newspaper clippings, and should be no more than ten pages. Attach your card or contact information to the packet.

  If possible, compile information about the impact of specific issues on the official's district or state. Do not compile a long list of statistics that will be difficult to remember. Instead, prepare a few dramatic numbers or anecdotes to illustrate your points. Collect recent local news articles that illustrate the issue. Like most people, elected officials are more likely to remember examples conveyed in human and personal terms.

- To encourage elected officials to support a specific immigration issue, present materials that clearly articulate your position, using specific case examples when possible.
- Know the counterarguments and the weaknesses in your position and be ready to respectfully respond to any questions or disagreements.
- Make sure everyone in your group is prepared. Brief everyone attending the meeting and make sure they have any written materials (biographical profiles of legislators and their views, etc.) to review well ahead of time.
- Be organized. Determine before the meeting each participant's role, who will discuss what, and in what order participants will speak.
- If you are part of a larger group or coalition, meet ahead of time. Everyone must agree before the meeting on your group's central message and your request of the legislator. Resolve any differences before the meeting.

MAKING THE PRESENTATION

- Be on time. Begin by introducing yourselves and explaining why you asked for the meeting. Confirm how long the meeting will be and adjust your presentation if you find out that you will have more or less time than you were told originally.
- Present your concerns simply and directly. Get to your bottom line immediately. Be brief, direct, courteous, and positive. Do not assume that the person with whom you are meeting has any prior knowledge of the subject. Presentation of each topic roughly should follow the outline below and should be informed by the messages you already have developed:

     Background: Explain the issue in the simplest possible terms.

Impact: Explain how the issue directly affects your community or the group you represent. If possible, include someone in your delegation who is directly affected by the issue.

Recommendation: Indicate what you would like the official to do. If you want the official to support a specific issue, explain how your community has been impacted, and the consequences in concrete terms if, for example, Congress does not pass effective and fair immigration reform. Finally, ask your official to support legislation that would authorize the reform you support.

Important Point: Remember NOT to do all of the talking. It is equally, if not more, important to know the official's position as it is for him or her to know yours. If you do all of the talking, it will be difficult for you to know where he or she stands. So make sure you give the official the opportunity to ask questions or state his or her opinions. Ask questions. Often the official will appreciate the opportunity to be heard.

- Do not argue with the official or his or her staff. Politely answer questions and concerns, but if you disagree, make your point and move on. Remember, you are meeting with the official or staff person to develop a relationship and inform him or her about your positions on issues. Do not disagree or debate among yourselves in front of the official—save that for after the meeting.

- If you do not know the answer to a question, say so, and promise to get back with the answer. Be sure to follow up with your answer as quickly as possible after the meeting.

- Don't use jargon. Remember that your official deals with dozens, if not hundreds, of issues each week, each with its own "language."

- Thank the official if he or she has been supportive. Officials get thanked far less often than they get criticized. Your official will appreciate your recognition.
- Be sure to ask for the official's support. If the official already is very supportive, ask him or her to take a leadership role.

FOLLOWING UP AFTER THE MEETING

- Send a note thanking the official or staff person for meeting with you. Briefly summarize the main points of the meeting.
- Remember to follow up with responses to any questions the official or staff person asked but you could not answer at the time, or with materials that were requested.
- Do not think of the meeting as an isolated event. Although you may not have a face-to-face meeting again for some time, invite the official to speak at an event or meeting. Think of other ways to maintain the relationship you have initiated.
- Report back to colleagues and others in your community. These reports are invaluable in developing strategies and tracking officials' positions on important issues.

COMMUNICATING EFFECTIVELY

We live in a complicated world and daily face complicated issues. One of the easiest ways to talk about an issue that conveys what you want to say in a strong, clear, and convincing way is to use "talking points." Talking points are notes or an outline that you write for yourself to help you frame your comments. You will be better prepared if you have thought through what you want to say and how you want to say it and don't repeat yourself. Talking points help you to do just that: They outline an issue in the simplest and strongest way and help you effectively make your point.

WORKING WITH OTHERS

Working with other organizations will expand your group's power and influence. Building a coalition (a group of groups) in your community is one of the most effective ways to advocate in support of an issue. Oftentimes, the more diverse the membership of your coalition, the more powerful your group will be. For example, a coalition made up of community, union, and business groups has the potential to achieve more than a group working on its own.

WAYS TO WORK IN THE COMMUNITY

- **Hold a neighborhood meeting.** Neighborhood meetings are great opportunities to tell people about your organization or an important issue. Invite friends, family members, coworkers, and members of community groups and anybody else who might be interested. If possible, serve snacks and refreshments, or make it a potluck.

  Show a video, read a short article, or invite a guest speaker, and then have a discussion afterward. Include a direct action for attendees to take after the meeting, such as writing letters to elected officials or committing to bringing a friend to the next meeting. Don't forget to pass around a sign-up sheet so that interested people can provide their names and contact information if they want more information.

- **Set up a table.** Watch out for concerts, festivals, rallies, picnics, fairs, and other events in your community and set up a table to display your organization's work. Staff your table with friendly representatives and bright and clear signs. Provide a sign-up sheet, informational flyers, handouts, petitions to sign, and postcards to send to legislators so that each passerby can get involved. Also distribute information where people gather, such as parks and Laundromats.

- **Use libraries and community facilities.** Public spaces are used by many people, and some include display cases available to local organizations. While you may be unable to promote a specific piece of legislation, create an interesting informational display to educate people about an issue. Set it up for a holiday, special event, or for no special reason at all, but be sure to always include the name of your group or coalition and contact information so that people can obtain more information and become involved.

- **Reach out to high school students.** Reach out to youth and youth organizations to get them involved. For example, a youth group that volunteers at a local soup kitchen may agree to write letters to legislators in support of just immigration reform. In addition, some issues fit nicely with a school's desire for their students to become actively involved in community projects, including pro-immigrant activities. Reach out to your local school and PTA to see how they can be involved in your work.

BEYOND YOUR COMMUNITY

One way to get your point of view out beyond your community is to work with the media. Call into radio stations that your community listens to in order to get the word out about your organization, coalition, or specific issue. Find out which newspaper reporters cover the issues relevant to your group, and contact them.

CONCLUSION

Immigration has made us a strong and great country. Our nation's public policies on immigration will either open us to a great new future, keep the legacy of the past alive, or close down the future, creating an environment that conflicts with our history and our founding—one that makes the words of Lady Liberty untrue.

It is my prayer that you, the reader, will better understand the immigration process, its difficulties and challenges, that you will pledge to help family, friends, and/or yourself to enjoy the fruits that the United States of America would offer to those who would join her.

Index

Acknowledgments

As always, I want to thank my family for their patience and love for me.

Thank you, Cristina Pérez, for providing a foreword and, more important, for introducing me to the team at the Immigrant Legal Resource Center (ILRC), without whom this book wouldn't have been possible. The ILRC is so well known among immigration activists that I have to be thankful for being blessed by their great work; an entire team of people dedicated to our country and legacy of being a welcoming nation has birthed this book. Eric Cohen, Kathy Brady, Angie Junck, Nora Privatera, Mark Silverman, and Sally Kinoshita have all contributed to the text. A special thanks to Judith Golub; without her leadership, this work would not exist.

And, finally, to my friends at Simon & Schuster, beginning with Judith Curr, Johanna Castillo, and Amy Tannenbaum.

About the Author

THE REVEREND LUIS CORTÉS JR. is the president and CEO of Esperanza USA, the largest Hispanic faith-based community development corporation in the country. In January 2005, he was featured as one of *Time* magazine's "25 Most Influential Evangelicals."

THE IMMIGRANT LEGAL RESOURCE CENTER
WWW.ILRC.ORG

HELPING IMMIGRANTS CLAIM THE FUTURE

Since 1979 the Immigrant Legal Resource Center (ILRC) has been a national leader in immigrant rights. We work to help our country value the contributions of immigrants, treat immigrants fairly and with dignity and respect, and provide equal rights to all people, regardless of their immigration status. The ILRC's pro-immigrant education, advocacy, and empowerment work help immigrants be more active in the democratic process in this country.

Although we do not handle the individual cases of any immigrants, we do work in the following three areas to help immigrants increase their ability to understand and address the laws and policies that affect their daily lives:

- **Civic Participation**—Working with immigrants to help them participate in the democratic process through programs such as naturalization, leadership development, and voter education.
- **Policy and Advocacy**—Engaging in advocacy with and education of government officials and governmental agencies, the media, and others on policies that impact immigrants including immigration law, health care access, and safety.
- **Technical Assistance**—Providing training, materials, written guides, outreach, and education on immigration law and policy.

To learn more about the ILRC, please visit us at www.ilrc.org.